# Becoming a Marines

## The Definitive Guide to Marine Corps Officer Candidate School

A special thanks to Gabriel Coeli is deserved here. His writing expertise and knowledge of the USMC transformed the incoherent ramblings of former candidates (who are many things, but novelist is not among them) into the tour de force you now have the privilege of reading. The subtitle is truth in advertising. This really is the definitive guide to Marine Corps Officer Candidate School (you're welcome by the way).

To use an already overused cliché, we couldn't have done it with you. Thanks Gabe.

# Table of Contents

# Disclaimer

You're about to become a candidate who will attempt to join the United States Marine Corps, so you are about to do business with a government. That said, you should get used to reading fine print as early as possible. Here goes nothing:

**Legal Notice**

**This book is the sole intellectual property of the authors, is under copyright, and is only authorized for personal use. It is illegal to amend, distribute, sell, or use any portion of this book for commercial purposes without the explicit consent of the authors.**

*Translation:* Please don't change, sell or steal our words without our permission.

**Disclaimer Notice**

**This book is for educational purposes only. The authors neither express nor imply warranties of any kind, and no content herein should be construed as legal or medical advice. By reading this book, the reader agrees to hold the authors free of all liability for losses, direct or indirect, incurred resulting from use of the information contained within this book, including but not limited to errors, omissions, or inaccuracies.**

*Translation:* This book is for education only. If 100% of our readers use the information correctly, 99.999% of our readers will benefit from it. Everyone is different, and there is no accounting for East or West. We are not lawyers or doctors, so consider yourself notified. If you hurt yourself with our workout program or accidentally stab yourself with the office supplies we told you to buy, that's on you, not us.

## Medical Disclaimer Notice

**This book is not designed to replace professional medical advice and was written for a general audience. Please consult a doctor before beginning any exercise or nutritional program, especially if you suffer any pre-existing medical conditions. Use of the content herein constitutes agreement on the reader's part to accept all ensuing risk and to hold harmless the authors against any damages or legal action.**

*Translation:* In case you missed it, this is a nice way to restate the fact that we are not doctors. The workout and nutrition plan in this book are scientifically solid and researched to the best of our judgment, experience, knowledge and ability, but we can't be held liable for any adversity you may experience by following our advice. *Please talk to a doctor before you start any workout or nutrition program,* especially if you suffer from any allergies or existing medical conditions. We wrote this book to get you whole and healthy – so there is nothing more important to us (and you, for that matter) than staying whole and healthy. Make that the #1 mission priority and please exercise your best judgment.

# Introduction

*"Some people live an entire lifetime and wonder if they have made a difference to the world. The Marines don't have that problem."*

-President Ronald W. Reagan

So, you have decided to take for yourself the mantle of one of the most legendary titles in history: Officer of Marines. It is a long, storied path to leading some of the world's most elite warfighters. Congratulations on making this decision. Despite the inflated bonuses and less-demanding training of the other four branches of military service, you have opted to join America's premier fighting organization – for pride, for prestige and for honor.

But let's not get ahead of ourselves with the congratulations – you have not earned the title of "Marine" yet, much less "Officer of Marines." Unlike the other branches of service, who designate you as an airman, sailor or soldier the minute you arrive at basic training or candidate school, you don't become a Marine until you overcome physical torment, mental anguish and the ten-week dark night of the soul that is Officer Candidate School (OCS.)

That is where this book, *Becoming an Officer of Marines,* comes in. In these pages, you will find the full OCS training schedule, a detailed course overview and a full pre-ship workout and nutrition program alongside hard-earned wisdom from Marines, candidates and officers who have gone before you. The combination of real-life lessons learned and physical and mental preparation will ensure that you not only survive at OCS, but that you *thrive* at OCS.

The authors of this book both completed their own crucibles – one at OCS in Quantico and one at enlisted boot camp at Marine Corps Recruit Depot in San Diego. All of the contributors of advice, information and stories are from former OCS candidates: Some of them were prior enlisted, some had zero military experience. Some made it through, some didn't – for one reason or another. Some are since retired from the Marine Corps and others are still active. The common thread is that they all remember doing as much research as possible to learn all they could before showing up – but they knew there was *something* missing.

That is what this book is: The missing link. It is not an official guide that your Officer Selection Officer (OSO) will give you, and it is not a flowery propaganda piece written by an advertising agency and published by the government to be as persuasive – and devoid of real content – as possible. This book contains information you can only find in one place in the world – not on the Internet, not in books, but from the mouths of veterans who undertook the challenges themselves. *Becoming an Officer of Marines* will give you a rare behind-the-scenes glimpse of what it is *really* like at OCS – everything you want to know, but no one will tell you. The goal of this book to remove as many surprises as possible for you as you undergo your transformation into an Officer of Marines.

Before we get started, there are two words of warning. Here is the first: New commanding officers have come and gone through Quantico in recent years, and it is possible that some things have changed since some of the contributors to this book attended OCS, albeit slightly. Things may change before the next class starts – in the Marine Corps, everything is subject to change, so you must learn to "adapt, improvise and overcome." However, you can count on 95% of the core OCS regimen remaining the same throughout the years – the Marines don't fix what ain't broke, and OCS ain't broken. The finest military officers in the world have come out of Quantico for more than a century.

The second word of warning: This book may seem, at times, to contain a collection of horror stories so terrible, so vicious and so frightening that any normal, sane person would run for the hills. So be it.  Yet, if the descriptions of torture, angst and sorrow you find in these pages excite you, you are the right person for the job – not because you are a masochist, but because you enjoy the unique thrill of overcoming true adversity.  Make no mistake – you will suffer.  You will suffer, you will reach your limits, and you will break down.  It is a critical part of the rite of passage – no hero's journey is complete without having been utterly devastated.

When you are at your lowest point, you will come to a point that all Marines know intimately – a place burned deep into the recesses of their memories.  Every muscle and nerve in your body will cry out at once to stop, to rest, to get relief.  You will have failed, and will have had your spirit shattered into pieces.  You will have the option to say, "enough is enough."  You will have the option to quit.  You will have the option to lie there in the mud, broken and defeated, and refuse to train.

If you decide to quit, the torture will stop.  No one will scream in your face, spraying spittle from their lips into your eyes.  No one will subject you any further to sleepless nights, endless death marches and psychological games that provoke a fury so deep it seems to emanate from your bones.  You will get a paycheck and a plane ticket home.  Once home, you will face your friends and family and tell them that you did not have what it took to become an Officer of Marines.  You will go back to the way things were, getting dressed in normal clothes, driving in a normal car through normal traffic to a normal job.

You will wake up each morning for the rest of your normal life, stand in front of the mirror, and struggle to look yourself in the eye.

However, when you hit rock bottom – when you find the absolute nadir of hope, and the absolute end of your physical, mental, emotional and spiritual resources – if you can reach within yourself to find those corners of your soul where the reserves of your deepest resolve reside, you will realize that you can overcome OCS. You can overcome *anything*. Your instructors have taught you everything you need to rebuild yourself. You can then choose to pull yourself up, claim your title, and in doing so, go on to become a model of strength and wisdom who will lead and inspire not only fighting men and women, but Americans everywhere.

The choice will be yours. Make the right one.

# Taking the First Steps

*"You are part of the world's most feared and trusted force. Engage your brain before you engage your weapon."*

-General James "Mad Dog" Mattis

## GETTING ACCEPTED TO OCS

Before we get too far ahead of ourselves, let's cover one of the most difficult – but least talked-about – steps in becoming an Officer of Marines: Getting accepted to OCS. Some officers will tell you that they just showed up and shipped off, while others had to fight through remedial physical training and a maze of administrative and bureaucratic red tape. It can be quite a hurdle to overcome, but it pales in comparison to what you will face at OCS. Nevertheless, there are steps you can take to ensure that the application process goes smoothly.

### Help Your OSO Help You

Your Officer Selection Officer (OSO) is a human being like any other, and getting to know him or her and making yourself useful will help your own process along. Keep in consistent contact with them – it's your job to do so, not the other way around – and foster a good relationship with them. You don't have to call and text them every day – a simple e-mail or phone call once every couple of weeks will suffice. They will keep you updated on any emergent changes or needs that, if quickly resolved, will increase your chances of being accepted.

### Don't Get Tattoos

Regardless of your personal feelings on tattoos – especially in the Marine Corps, where it's practically a rite of passage for many fighting men and women – the big brass don't want officers to have tattoos.  If you have any tattoos that are visible in Physical Training (PT) gear, which is the uniform with olive green shirt and shorts, you maybe outright disqualified.  Even if you have a tattoo no one will ever see in uniform, you will have to get a waiver – and too many waivers can shut down your chances of getting in.  Getting a waiver also can take a long time, depending on how busy the brass is at any given moment, so it could delay your acceptance.

## Fake It 'Til You Make It

You are hoping to become an Officer of Marines – and once you have dozens or even hundreds of lives in your hands, you won't be doing stupid things like taking illegal drugs or drunk driving.  Start holding yourself to that standard now.  Not only does "someday never come," if you do any of these things while in the application process and get caught, kiss your dream of becoming an Officer of Marines goodbye.  There are waivers available for past drug use or legal trouble, but only in special circumstances, and the Marines won't take a candidate that needs too many waivers.  The simpler and cleaner your application, the easier it is to be selected.

## Focus on Physical Fitness

This book has you covered on all the preparations you will need to make in order to get in prime physical condition – just flip to Chapter 8.  You can't skimp on fitness right now – the higher your score on the Physical Fitness Test (PFT), the easier it will be to get accepted to OCS.  You can be impressive in every other way – a member of Mensa, a *wunderkind* leader and a direct blood descendant of Chesty Puller – but if you can't muster up a good run time, the Marines will kindly point you in the direction of the Air Force recruiter.

**PREPARING YOUR FAMILY**

No matter what, you are going to have to prepare your family for the fact that you are planning to become an Officer of Marines. They will be exceedingly proud of you, but their minds will also jump immediately to the worst-case scenarios, so you need to make sure they have the information they need to rest as easily as possible at night.

**Talking to Your Spouse**

If you are married, make sure your spouse is fully on board with your decision. Not only will you be away for a long time with only short breaks to see him or her when you go to OCS and The Basic School (TBS) immediately thereafter, military life takes a lot of adjustment. Your spouse needs to be prepared for the potential of multiple deployments – and occasional seven-day work weeks and twenty-hour work days back in garrison. The website Circle of Moms has a great roundup of the 25 best Military Family blogs your spouse can read in order to get an understanding of what military life will be like.

**Answering Your Family's Questions**

Your family will likely have a lot of questions. You should do your best to answer these questions and put their minds at ease as much as possible before you leave for OCS – and direct any questions they have while you are gone to the OSO.

Here are four of the most common questions your family will need answers for:

1. *Can we visit you?* The answer to this question is that you can only see your family when you are on liberty, which you won't get until Week 3, and which usually only lasts from Saturday evening through Sunday afternoon. It is

great to see your family, but some candidates find it a big distraction, especially if there is stress back home, so it might be best for some candidates if families wait until graduation day to make the trip.

2. *Can we call you?* The only time you will have access to your personal cell phone is during liberty. Make sure your family knows that you will call them – and then follow up and be sure to call them every week. Of course, if there is an emergency, your family will be able to reach you at any point in your training by contacting their local Red Cross. The Red Cross understands the procedures by which they need to get a hold of a candidate in training and will take care of everything on behalf of your family.

3. *Is the training dangerous?* Be careful answering this one. Yes, the training is dangerous, and Marine OCS was in the news five or six years ago because of candidate deaths. However, the professionals that run the show over there know what they are doing, and will do everything in their power to make sure you are not seriously injured or killed. If your family is concerned you will be low crawling under barbed wire and machine gun fire and jumping out of helicopters, you can gently disabuse them of this notion now – eventually, you will get to do these kinds of things, but OCS is not where you do the "fun stuff."

4. *Who should I contact if there is a problem?* Let them know that your OSO is their point of contact for any non-emergency situations or questions that arise while you are in training. Your family needs to know that they should never contact staff at Quantico, VA, including (and especially) your commanding officer.

16

## Mail

Your family will want to do all they can to support you while you are in training, and you shouldn't turn them down. It's important to them to feel like they are there for you as you undertake this great challenge. One of the best things you can ask your family to do is send you mail. While in OCS, you won't have much time to read their letters, but when you get them, it will make a huge difference. The amount of stress you are under, combined with an environment full of screaming, hostile military instructors, will make you a big huge emotional squish the first time you get a note of encouragement from your Mom or Dad. Knowing they are there for you and thinking of you can help get you through tough times. Ten weeks doesn't seem like a long time until you're two weeks into training – then, the prospect of two more hours, much less two more months, can seem like an eternity in the lake of fire.

Your family may want to ensure you get their mail as quickly as possible by sending it as Overnight Mail, but this actually won't help – all the mail has to go through a review process, so it will still be held up for some time before it reaches you.

One important caveat: Ensure that they do not send any kind of food or goods to you while you are at OCS – letters only. Food, gum and other treats are considered contraband, so it will likely get thrown away, and may cause you to catch some flak from your instructors. A handy rule to tell your family is to send nothing larger than a standard letter, with nothing in the envelope but paper. Anything else will be flagged and confiscated.

If you receive any contraband whatsoever in your mail, report it immediately and turn it in to your instructors. You will not get in trouble for turning it in, but you could be kicked out of OCS if you attempt to hide it.

The address where your family can send mail is:

Candidate (Last Name), (First Name), (Middle Initial)
___ Company, ___Platoon
Officer Candidates School
2189 Elrod Avenue
Quantico, Virginia 22134-5033


Once your family is prepared and your application process has gone smoothly, you will be ready to leave. The next chapter has you covered on everything you will need to know for the reporting process. Read on!

# Reporting to OCS

*"The journey of a thousand miles begins with a single step."*

- Lao Tzu

You have been selected as a candidate for OCS, and now you are off to Quantico. One of the first things you will learn is how difficult the military makes what should otherwise be relatively simple tasks. Welcome to reporting in.

A quick note, here: The madness you've heard about doesn't get started for a few days. In fact, when you first show up, military personnel will be quite courteous with you, and will stay largely invisible except to direct you where to go and what to do.

### Arriving at the Airport

First things first – you are going to have a bad time if you show up looking "nasty." You need to be in what the Marines consider "appropriate civilian attire," which means trousers (usually khakis,) a tucked-in collared shirt (polo or button-up) and dress shoes. When you first fly in to Ronald Reagan Washington National Airport, look for the Marine Liaison team (you can spot them by their Service "C," or Charlie, uniform) to show up around 1600 (that's 4:00 PM for the uninitiated.)

If you show up at a different airport than Ronald Reagan – or don't get to Ronald Reagan by 1700, you may have to get your own transportation to Quantico, and it may not be reimbursable. Use the SuperShuttle at the rental car area at Ronald Reagan to save some money. If you don't ride over with the Marine Liaisons, make sure to call the Officer of the Day (OOD) at OCS at 703-432-6050.

**Travel Tips**

Make sure you save all your travel receipts – even for food. The administrative clerk won't actually need your meal expenses, because you will be paid a *per diem* allowance, but it is good practice to save all of your receipts when you are traveling on the government's dime. If you lose one, you will have a devil of a time getting it reimbursed, especially since the Marine Corps Financial Disbursers tightened up the rules on lost receipts a few years ago.

If you decided to take a car rather than a plane, show up at OCS between 1600 and 2000 – because if you show up at any other time, they will turn you away. Also, you will need to have a driver's license, registration and proof of insurance to even get on base, so double check that you have everything before you show up.

Lastly, if for any weather-related reason you are unable to report on time (say your plane is grounded, for instance) call the OOD immediately and maintain communication with him or her throughout the duration of the delay. If this causes you to be late, you may need to get your own transportation from the airport to Quantico – on your own dime. However, don't forget about the SuperShuttle that runs to Quantico out of the rental car area at Ronald Reagan Airport. It can save you a bundle over renting a car or taking a cab.

**The Packing List**

Your OSO will give you an official packing list of everything you need to bring to OCS. One of the most common questions candidates have before they take off is, "Do I need to bring all this stuff?" Read this carefully: Yes. Read this carefully, again: Yes.

If your OSO tells you to bring it, you bring it. Plain and simple. Assuming you know better than a black-and-white order you have been given is a recipe for disaster later in your Marine Corps career, so get used to it now.

If you want to overachieve and bring more than the packing list calls for, on the other hand, you are more than welcome to do that, so long as you don't bring anything that is officially designated contraband by the CO of Quantico.

Here is a comprehensive packing list. Again, ensure you have everything on the packing list your OSO gives you – then cross-reference against this one and feel free to bring anything else you read about here.

- 2 sets of civilian clothing (trousers, collared shirt, belt, shoes)
- 2 pairs of black dress socks (solid black)
- 2 pairs of combat boot socks (the Thorlo brand is a good one.)
- 1 pair of Bates Lights garrison boots (break these in before you get there)
- 2 pairs of supportive boot insoles (the SuperFeet brand is good)
- 3 pairs white running socks
- 2 pairs of slightly broken-in running shoes in excellent condition.
- 4 extra skivvie shirts
- 4 extra PT shorts
- 6 pairs of underwear
- 6 sports bras (only if you're female, obviously. Gentlemen, those aren't within regs for you.)
- 1 travel towel
- Toothbrush
- Toothpaste
- Two razors (you won't be able to buy a new one for two weeks, or possibly longer)

- 1 can shaving cream
- 1 stick deodorant
- 1 bottle body wash
- 2 tubes Chap Stick
- 1 large bottle hair gel (for females only, to assist with fixing bun flyaways.)
- 1 manicure kit (both men and women – helpful on inspection day)
- 1 bag to hold your hygiene gear
- 1 bottle of lotion
- 1 bottle of sunscreen
- 2 notebooks (the Rite in the Rain 3x5 are great)
- 1 box of black pens (never blue ink) – erasable, if possible
- 2 red pens – erasable, if possible
- 1 box of mechanical pencils
- 2 permanent markers (Sharpie Rub-a-Dub)
- 2 wide-tip permanent markers (again, head with Sharpie and you won't go wrong)
- 1 small pair of scissors
- 1 red LED headlamp (red light won't destroy your night vision)
- 1 waterproof watch (no shiny metal – best to buy a black tactical watch with Velcro)
- $500 in cash
- ATM/Debit Card
- Driver's License/Identification
- 4 rolls of 1" white athletic tape (you will come to know this as candidate tape)
- 1 roll of electrical tape
- 1 roll of duct tape
- All pertinent medical, dental and immunization records
- 1 box of 1-quart Ziploc bags
- 1 box of 1-gallon Ziploc bags

## Gifting

If you have the money and extra room in your luggage, *bring extra supplies and gear.* Someone will forget something important, and if you have the ability to give them a gift and save their ass – especially early on – you will earn brownie points with your soon-to-be peers. Notice that phrasing: "Give them a gift." That doesn't mean loaning it to a fellow candidate, or expecting someone to pay you back at some point. You give a gift because it is the right thing to do. Anyway, it's not completely altruistic: It is always better to be owed a favor than money – best to learn to start stocking up favors from your friends, colleagues, peers and especially your nemeses now, especially if you want to make it past the rank of Captain someday.

# The First Few Days

*"Paperwork will ruin any military force."*

- Lieutenant General Lewis "Chesty" Puller

See that quote above? It's from Lewis B. Puller, the Marine's Marine, also known as "Chesty" — a man so steeped in legend and mythology in the Marine Corps that you will see and hear his quotes absolutely everywhere. Fun fact of the day: There is no way to tell if he said half of what he said; myths are funny like that. We can't even vouch for the veracity of the above quote. But you will come to know and love Chesty like he was your own CO — guaranteed.

Back to the task at hand: Did you think you wrapped up all the paperwork with your OSO? Think again. Welcome to the first few days at OCS — processing, procedure and paperwork as far as the eye can see.

The mission of OCS is to "train, screen and evaluate candidates, who must demonstrate a high level of leadership potential and commitment to success in order to earn a commission." In plain English, it's to weed out those who cannot hack it. They have only a few short weeks to make this determination for a lot of candidates, so you might think they turn it up to 11 when you first step off the bus, much like you may have seen (or experienced first-hand) at boot camp with the yellow footprints. Not so. Not yet, at any rate.

**How It Is**

As you nervously anticipate the day you actually pack your stuff, get on the plane, and fly out for a few weeks of fun in Quantico, VA, you may have built it up in your mind, thinking of the stories you've heard from people who have been there before and getting more and more anxious as the big day gets closer.  This is not lost on the fine Marines at OCS.  In fact, they have an ingenious way of ensuring that anxiety builds up to a maximum crescendo before the fun starts.  How?  Things are nice, smooth and quiet the first two or three days after you report in.  Marines are not overly friendly with you, but no one is yelling at you and you will not be rushed or harried.  You will get a non-commissioned officer (NCO, usually a sergeant) who will be your platoon guide, meaning they just shepherd you around from place to place, like chow and the Installation Personnel Administration Center (IPAC.)  These first few days are just in-processing, where you get your medical check, get your gear, shuffle through a mountain of forms, statements of understanding, receipts and other paperwork.

Now, don't feel bad about yourself if you find that the first few days are mentally draining, especially since you've got a lot of downtime where you have to sit there and read the little red book issued to you.  The red book is filled with all the leadership traits and other required knowledge (most or all of which you should already know or be very familiar with – see Chapters 6 and 7 of this guide for preparation.)  You aren't allowed to talk or fall asleep, so you will be excruciatingly *bored*.  You are left alone with your thoughts as you are shuffled from place to place, which, by the way, you will learn is called "Hurry up and wait" and will be the standard way of life for the duration of your stay at OCS – and your career in the Marine Corps.  Even if you end up Chairman of the Joint Chiefs of Staff someday, you will find yourself rushing to the White House to give a briefing to the President, only to be told you have to wait while the Big Dog irons out some political gaffe the Press Secretary made on the Sunday morning shows the weekend previous.  It never stops – you can get angry, get heartburn and high blood pressure and let it give you a heart attack and an untimely death at a young age, or you can learn to be Zen about it and enjoy any free time you get. We strongly recommend the latter.

## The Game Begins

After a few days of "hurry up and wait," the Big Day comes when you get the "welcome speech" from the commanding officer of OCS and you are introduced to your Sergeant Instructors. They are not yelling at you yet. In fact, the Commanding Officer (CO) is usually low-key, exceedingly professional and to the point. He or she might even congratulate you on getting this far, but only to make the next point that that is the last time you will be given any positive feedback. He or she will tell everyone that they are to pick up all their gear, and everyone is required to go out and make a head call (this is Marine-speak for using the bathroom,) whether you need to or not. Take his advice and squeeze out whatever you can. You will be happy you did.

The CO will then explain that should you have decided in the last few days, hours, or minutes that OCS and the Marines just aren't for you. You will get the option to simply walk down the hall and form a line where you are directed. *This is not a trick.* No one will ask you any questions or try to talk you out of it. They will not yell at you or punish you. They will simply give you a plane ticket and let you go home and enjoy the rest of your summer.

If you were thinking that after all the work these candidates have done to get selected, all the effort they put in to prepare for OCS, then travel to get to Quantico, no one would chicken out at the last second – right? Wouldn't they at least try?

Think again. Someone always takes the CO up on his or her offer – and sometimes it is as many as eight or ten candidates. They walk down the hallway, heads hanging in shame. It takes a day or two to get their paperwork done and get them a plane ticket home, but once they have gone and stood in the line, they can't turn back.

They are segregated from the rest of the candidates, although you'll eventually see them off to the side at other tables at chow time. Unlike if you get injured or fail too many tests and get kicked out, if you quit OCS, you never get to come back. *Never.*

Now, when this time is upon you, you may find yourself thinking that magical, two-word phrase: *Fuck this.* Welcome to being a Marine, and a human being. If you don't even consider it, you're probably a little off in the head. Nearly everyone considers it, and that's the whole point. It's the deep breath before the plunge. But consider this: If you can't hack it after only a couple of days of boredom – that is, if you can't summon the intestinal fortitude to stick with your decision after all of the effort you've put in and commitments you've made, you won't make it through the rest of OCS. The CO is doing these candidates a favor. If you want to become an officer of Marines, you don't need that generosity. Stand fast – this is the first volley fired in the great game that is OCS – and prepare yourself for the nightmare headed your way.

# Embrace the Suck

*"We don't promise you a rose garden."*

- Marine Corps Recruiting Poster circa 1970

In case you didn't know this, the word "Marines" doesn't actually have anything to do with the fact that this fighting organization is naval infantry, or designed for amphibious warfare. It's actually an acronym that stands for "Many Americans Running Into Never Ending Shit." The shit may never end, but it definitely has a beginning – and for you, it is right here, right now on the day your platoon "picks up" at OCS.

Of course, we're making a joke about the Marine Corps' name – but not the shit. Throughout your military career, you will constantly run into something first observed by Prussian General Carl von Clausewitz, the author of *On War* (a treatise which, if you have not read, you should.) Clausewitz wrote, "Everything in war is very simple, but the simplest thing is difficult. The difficulties accumulate and end by producing a kind of friction that is inconceivable unless one has experienced war."

The modern Marine Corps has an updated term for "friction." Nowadays, we just say, "embrace the suck." It means, "The situation is shitty. Deal with it."

Get embracing, candidate. In this chapter, you will find a rundown on the *worst* elements of OCS. Let's get started.

**THE GAME**

If you skipped ahead in this book to any section, there is a good chance this is it. As previously mentioned, OCS is a game. It is you versus OCS, and they are doing everything they can to make sure you don't make it to graduation.  Here is why:  If you can't hold yourself together in the face of someone verbally tearing you down and assigning you essays, just imagine what a Taliban mortar will do to your self-esteem.

## Sergeant Instructors

Now that we've mentioned the Sergeant Instructors, let's get one thing clear.  If you aren't prior enlisted and have never encountered a Drill Instructor before, there really is no preparing for Sergeant Instructors.  You've seen it on TV or YouTube, but until you experience it firsthand, their entire modality of existence beggars belief.  They will convince you that they hate you and want you to die.  In fact, there will be times you are certain they are indeed about to murder you, as they will often threaten.  We would say that you should be mentally prepared for this as much as possible, but there is no preparation you can make, except to realize that this is a game, and to never forget that Sergeant Instructors are incredibly good actors.  At the end of the day, that is all they are.

There are many Marines that believe in order to become a Drill Instructor or Sergeant Instructor, you must have some base level of sadism in your soul – some sociopathic ruthlessness and love of bullying, some place in your central processing unit where the empathy circuit fried out, leaving only brutality, fury and vicious cruelty.  It's not true – but that is a testament to how good these people are.  While you may come to believe that Sergeant Instructors really are hateful, motherless degenerates that spawned in some hellish swamp, you just need to remember that they are trying to defeat you.  If they succeed, they have weeded out an unfit commander who will only go on to get themselves and their people killed, and potentially lose a battle – or even a war.

We told you this was a "game," but that doesn't mean it's child's play. The stakes here are life and death – for you, your future subordinates, the entire Marine Corps, and for the existential security of the United States of America.

**The Rules of the Game**

Here are the rules of the game:

1. You always lose.
2. In the event that you win, the rules will change to ensure that you lose.

Everything you do is wrong. This is the whole point of OCS. Even if you do something right, they will find something wrong – or make something up and punish you anyway. They want to take people who are used to winning and succeeding in most everything they've ever done in life and make them fail over and over and over at the simplest tasks. Understand this: *OCS is not fair.* The Sergeant Instructors get to cheat as much as they want. Once you figure out how to win the game, they will change the rules so you fail again. You can always be faster and more intense – and get ready to hear that a lot: "Speed and intensity." Even if you do manage to do something right, you'll never do it with enough speed or intensity to satisfy the Sergeant Instructors. You lose and lose and lose, all the way up to the moment you've graduated and pinned on your butter bars. Until then, embrace the suck.

The point of the constant frustration and defeat is to sow chaos and discord in your soul. They want to see how you react when the world around you is crumbling and defeat is imminent. Do you respond to the situation and make the best of it, or react to your emotions and lose your military bearing?

## I Will Hold

During the Battle of Belleau Wood in France, fought in 1918 during World War I, First Lieutenant Clifton B. Cates ran into an impossibly large force of German soldiers. He sent a message to his commander saying this: "I have only two men out of my company and twenty out of some other company. We need support, but it is almost suicide to try to get it here as we are swept by machine gun fire and a constant barrage is on us. I have no one on my left and only a few on my right. I will hold."

*I will hold.*

The man faced overwhelming odds and certain death, and held it together, because he knew what he had to do, no matter the adversity. You know what happened to Lieutenant Cates? After his Marines exhausted their ammunition, they went to bayonets and hand-to-hand combat. They survived that battle, and over the next month, they (along with the rest of the Fifth Marine Division) defeated a German force that was five times as large. According to Marine Corps mythology, the retreating Germans reported to their superiors that the Marines fought like *Teufelshunde* –"Devil Dogs." Cates went on to become the 19th Commandant of the United States Marine Corps.

*I will hold.*

Never show emotion. Never show that you are angry, never show that you are stressed, never show that you are happy or sad. Never show that you are *human.* Hold the line. If the SI is in your face, screaming and yelling and you keep messing up and can't get it right, hold the line. *Do not* make a face, don't shake your head, don't even blink. Stay as calm as possible, think about what you are trying to do, and focus on that – no matter that the Sergeant Instructor does or says.

If you can maintain your bearing, the SI will eventually get bored with you and move on. Never crumble under pressure and never give up, no matter how bad the situation is – that is what they are looking for. The fact that you can't succeed does not matter. Hold the line.

The Sergeant Instructors will methodically test each person at some point. If you sound off, look straight ahead, stand up straight, and respond quickly and firmly (remember, it doesn't matter if you are right or wrong in your answer, as long as you are confident in how you do it), this is what they want to see, and they won't need to put a special amount of work into you.

*Their job is to defeat you.* They will search you out, find your weak point, and try to use it against you. If you start off on the right foot, they won't try hard. If you give them a reason, they will focus on you and your time at OCS will be hell.

### You Will Get Skylined

But do not skyline yourself on the first day! "Skyline" is a term from World War I, in which someone would stand on top of a high ridge (the "line" where the earth meets the sky in an enemy's field of vision) making them an easy target for a sniper or machine gun. You will eventually get skylined –through your own actions or someone else's – but if an SI learns your name out of sixty candidates on the first day because you seriously screwed the pooch, you might be in for a long few weeks unless you straighten up fast.

Finally, it is important to keep something in perspective. These Sergeant Instructors have dedicated their lives to service, and are some of the best instructors – and finest Marines – in the entire Corps. They have trained a lot of young Marines, to whom you will potentially be responsible for their well-being. Think of it from their perspective. They are salty (experienced) Marines who are picking from a group of college boys who will soon be out-ranking them and are supposed to be able to lead them. You're damn right they are going to take that responsibility seriously.

## Punishments

Unlike for enlistees at boot camp, they can't smoke you (call you up on the quarterdeck and hand out exercises as punishment.) That said, you may have to get your "packs inspected" a few times. This entails filling a pack with the required load and holding it out at arms' length so the SI can inspect it. Doesn't sound bad? Next time you are at the gym, latch onto a 25lb dumbbell and hold it out for 15 minutes. This doesn't happen often, but you might run into something like this once or twice if a group punishment is in order.

Individual punishment is a whole different ball game. Since they can't make you do mountain climbers till you puke, they give you essays. Yes, essays.

Here is the criteria for an essay:

- 300 word essays. That means 300, not 299, not 301.
- Only words with 4 or more letters count towards the 300.
- Each of those words that count must be underlined and numbered 1-300 with the number circled.
- You skip every other line (the space is used for numbers) and you have to flip your paper over so it can be read from a clipboard.
- If you have a grammar or typo, you fail and have to restart. You cannot have any cross-outs, lines, etc.
- It must be written in BLACK ink, not blue, not red.
- Violate any of the previous items, and you'll likely get another essay in addition to redoing the one you messed up.

There is only one part in a 24-hour day that you really have much time to write the essays: After lights out. After a day at OCS, your mind and body is worthless and it will become *very* hard to write sentences without mistakes. The first few days, you might only get two hours of sleep a night, and you may get more than one or two essays during that time. You will barely be able to keep your eyes open, and you will learn the true meaning of despair when you are on your fourth or fifth attempt and misspell word 295 of 300, look up at the clock and realize it is 2am, and you still have to get your gear ready and study for a test before 5 am rolls around. Count on it.

You *will* get an essay. If you do everything perfect, you will still get an essay. Remember how we said they will make you fail? One guy got an essay because the SI slapped a "spider" off his shoulder (there was no spider) and made him write about how he was "a lazy candidate and made the SI save his life from the poisonous spider". It's not a matter of "if", it's a matter of "when" and "how many".

# Schedule Overview

*"If you know the enemy and know yourself, you need not fear the result of a hundred battles. If you know yourself but not the enemy, for every victory gained you will also suffer a defeat. If you know neither the enemy nor yourself, you will succumb in ever battle."*

—Sun Tzu

During your time at OCS, you will be tested in three major areas: Leadership, Academics and Physical Fitness. Each of these are covered in a separate chapter in this book, but this chapter serves as a general overview of what you will focus on, and when. Think of it as a training schedule in greater detail. It is based on a schedule from 2008, which is a few years old, but to be truthful with you, this schedule likely hasn't changed much in a long time. As we've stated before, the finest military officers in the world have come out of Quantico for over a century.

## A Typical Day

We won't break down each and every day for you – we are just going to give you a general overview of the schedule, so you should know there are a few basic things that are going to happen every day (with a few exceptions.) You will get three meals, you will get time for personal hygiene and you will get to sleep. You will never get enough time to perform any of these things at a nice, leisurely pace – much less enjoy them – but you can count on these as the structure of your day. There is a saying at enlisted boot camp that goes, "Chow to chow, rack to rack, Sunday to Sunday." This means that your hourly, daily and weekly milestones (food, sleep and free time) are the best way to tell time – and get yourself through inordinately frustrating tasks, punishments or the grinding boredom that you will encounter from time to time. Everything else in the schedule – just like everything else in the Marine Corps – is "subject to change." Semper Gumby.

**Week One**

We've already covered the first few days of OCS, so suffice it to say that this is when you will get uniform issues, medical screenings, haircuts and your 782 gear issue (packs, field gear such as e-tools, etc.) During Week One, you will also learn how to make your bed (it's called a rack in the Corps) and begin combat first aid training, and if you're at winter OCS, you will learn cold weather injury prevention training. You will get the orientation from your commanding officer and pick up with your Sergeant Instructors, as covered earlier, then you will study interior guard procedures, basic military studies and military leadership, and customs and courtesies. You will get your weapon, you will begin learning close order drill, you will meet the chaplain, and you will learn how to "field day" your barracks.

## Week Two

Get ready for a whole lot of drill and physical training. This is the week when leadership billets get passed out (more on these later) and when you'll undergo the weapons performance test. You'll also study land navigation, military ceremony, local security and the fundamentals of offensive combat tactics. In the middle of the week, you will get a breakdown from your commander on what you will be evaluated on as a candidate – almost all of that should be in this book, but pay close attention. All commanders are different. Around that same time, you'll get a chance to make a PX call and buy any gear you need to keep going. Toward the end of the week, you'll learn more about tactics and gain some military field operations skills. You'll also get a primer on Marine Corps history and a class on fraternization – make *damn sure* to pay attention during that one. You'd be amazed how many senior enlisted Marines and officers lose their careers over fraternization.

At the end of the week (usually on Saturday) you'll have your first test, covering mostly drill and weapons – but anything you have learned at OCS thus far could show up. Take notes whenever you can and study up.

On Sunday, you'll learn how to conduct a march and how to set up a bivouac site. You'll also get a class on Equal Opportunity – racism, sexism and homophobia are totally unsatisfactory in the military, and you can kiss your career goodbye if you don't take Equal Opportunity seriously.

## Week Three

More land navigation, as well as classes on uniforms, more classes about fraternization (we told you it's serious) and good knowledge about decision-making using the OODA loop. At some point this week, usually Tuesday, you get your first "hump" – known as a conditioning hike – that lasts about four miles. This one isn't too bad, but there are humps coming up that will destroy a third or more of your platoon. Be prepared. You'll get another written exam on what you've learned thus far around this time.

Later, you'll go on to Marine Corps history again, visit the Marine Corps Uniform shop, learn to maintain your weapon and do another four-mile conditioning hike (usually on Thursday.) You'll learn about fire team organization and tactics, and then on Friday, you'll run the obstacle course. If you're not ready for this, it will screw you up, so make sure you follow the advice in Chapter 8 and get strong before you leave. You'll also get core values training, a suicide awareness class and you'll tour the National Museum of the Marine Corps. Saturday, you'll stand inspection for the Sergeant Instructors, then you'll head over for dress and service uniform purchase and fitting. If the Company Commander decides your platoon isn't too screwed up, you'll get liberty from Saturday evening to Sunday around 1900. If you're smart, you won't go screw off on the base somewhere; you'll find somewhere quiet, get something nice to eat and study up on Marine Corps history. When you get back, get your head in the game immediately. Week Four is coming for you.

## Week Four

First things first: You'll get a written exam on Marine Corps history on Monday morning. PT, then classes about substance abuse and domestic violence. More core values training, and classes about sexual misconduct. Monday night, you'll probably conduct night land navigation and compass training.

Next up, you've got a six-mile conditioning hike. Lucky you. You'll also get a chance to request mast with the Battalion Commander. This is not the time to bring up petty shit. However, if you have a serious problem and both the Sergeant Instructors and your company commander can't handle it – or you have seen a major breach of the law or policy and you don't trust your instructors or commander to take care of it – this is when you can let the Battalion CO know about it. *They will take this very seriously.* You better take it seriously, too. Request Mast is one of the most ancient rights in the Marine Corps, and you must honor it with your own Marines someday.

You'll spend some more time outdoors on Wednesday, then on Thursday you'll learn about the Law of Land War and the Code of Conduct. You'll also get classes on the Uniform Code of Military Justice – also known as the UCMJ. Thursday is the first day you perform peer evaluations, and you'll also get another SI inspection. Next up is more Marine Corps history, general training like weapons maintenance and PT, and then liberty on Saturday evening.

## Week Five

Monday morning you get your written exam on Leadership. Don't screw it up. After that, you'll get more classes on offensive combat tactics and combat signs and formations. You'll also get a class on the Marine Corps' mission and organization, and start learning some martial arts. Tuesday, you'll have a written exam on Tactics, then you'll get a course on combat. Wednesday is your Land Nav exam. You'll also get a class on Marine Corps history (there is a lot of it) and some more core values training. Around this time, you'll also run the *big* obstacle course – called the Confidence Course – and get a class on operations orders. Thursday, you will get a class on issuing and receiving orders, then more land navigation. Uniform fittings go down today, as well as more classes on combat. Friday it's the confidence course again, along with a platoon sergeant inspection. If you are screwed up during the inspection, don't expect to get liberty. On Saturday, you run a Physical Fitness Test – pull-ups, crunches and a three-mile run. This makes a huge difference to your score, so don't screw it up. You'll get more core values training, then leave on libo. Congratulations – you're halfway through.

## Week Six

This week will fly by – so enjoy it. You start off with training on moral leadership, the five-paragraph order, tactics, combat hunting and an examination on Night Land Navigation. You'll get some more martial arts on Tuesday, as well as more time in the field, studying squad movements. Thursday there will be a second peer evaluation, as well as a class on professional ethics and some more martial arts. Friday you'll come back from the field and do your next exam on Marine Corps history. After that, a class on sexual harassment, more martial arts, counseling from your instructors, then another platoon sergeant inspection prior to liberty.

## Week Seven

You start the week with an examination on operations orders, then you're off to core values training. You will get some administrative classes this week – hooray for paperwork – including orders processing, administrative out-processing, the DD-214 for those who are commissioning, the Leave and Earnings Statement and the commissioning process. Tuesday, you'll have another written examination on Leadership. Wednesday, it's off to an ethics discussion with the commander and the married candidates will get a brief on base housing before everyone gets a class on household effects and how to do the paperwork to move your things to TBS. Thursday is PT, PX and uniform fittings (you've probably lost a good amount of weight – fat and muscle – by this point) as well as another exam on Tactics. Friday, you'll get a class on leadership from the company commander, and you will get a Small Unit Leadership Exam. Saturday there will be more classes on leadership and you will get to fight other candidates with pugil sticks (which means it is payback time if you got a rough peer evaluation.) Then you get to go on liberty broken and bruised. Study up on general military studies – you have an exam on Monday.

**Week Eight**

Monday, you'll get a test on general military studies, as well as a class from the Sergeant Major on how to relate to senior enlisted Marines. You'll also get an orders processing class and take platoon pictures (in which you will – guaranteed – look awful.) After that, you'll get a motivational speech from a guest speaker. Tuesday is squad offensive tactics, ID cards and individual drill examinations. Wednesday is another Small Unit Leadership Examination, squad offensive tactics and a big conditioning hike. You're going to hike nine miles with a full kit, and it is going to kick off at 0300 – meaning you will be up at midnight. Embrace the suck. Thursday, it's your third go-around for peer evaluations, then a PX call and another guest speaker in the evening after chow. Friday is all drill and uniforms, and Saturday is counseling, PX, drill, a discussion with the commander about the meaning of your commission – which is highly motivating (though if you have struggled with motivation up until now, how are you still in the program?) and then on into libo. Of course, if you have screwed anything up to this point, you won't get libo – you'll get remediation instead.

## Week Nine

You're coasting, now. Almost all of the hard stuff is behind you. You are also past what is known as the "pressure cooker." You know you're close, so it's easy to get complacent – and in the Marine Corps, complacency kills. If anyone is going to get in serious trouble, this week will be when they do it, because they have let their guard down. Don't be that candidate.

Monday you will do an "end-of-course critique" (though it's a bit premature) and some classes on professional reading. You'll discuss ethics with the battalion commander and start administrative outprocessing. This is the day your families can buy tickets to Family Day, incidentally. Let them know. Tuesday, there's another uniforms issues and a run to the Cash Sales store, then you'll get another inspection – this time with the company commander on the parade deck. Expect this to take six hours or longer – your legs will *hurt*. Wednesday is a big PT day, with a log run and more pugil stick fighting. Some of you may also get to play around with a helicopter today – but we won't ruin the surprise.

On Thursday, you will receive your Eagle, Globe and Anchor. At this point, you have been given the symbol of the United States Marine Corps. Relish this moment – you will never forget it.

You will get a TBS orientation and a class on patterns of conflict, as well (it's a little anticlimactic after the ceremony – can't lie) then on Friday you'll continue TBS orientation in the morning and have your drill competition on the Parade Deck in the afternoon. This will take the entire afternoon. Saturday, you'll rehearse for graduation, then PT, then on to sweet, sweet liberty.

## Week Ten

Monday, you've got PT – specifically, the Medal of Honor run. Look forward to it – it's inspirational as hell. If you don't already have an ID card, you will get it today. Today or tomorrow, you'll stand an inspection in your camouflage utilities before the Battalion Commander (why not in service uniforms? A great question that we don't have the answer to.) One thing is for sure on Tuesday – you get rid of that awful candidate-grade 782 gear...at least until you get to TBS and see the hand-me-down garbage they have waiting for you to lug around. Wednesday you'll handle administrative stuff and do a motivational run with your battalion commander, which no matter how good of a runner you are, will probably break you off at the knees. Regardless, you're in good enough shape to make it through, so have confidence in yourself. Afterward, you head out for graduation and commissioning rehearsal, then you get a class with your battalion commander on being a Lieutenant of Marines. Afterward, you'll have a field meet – usually with a barbecue (and if you're lucky, the battalion CO or XO will cook.) On Thursday, you'll rehearse your commissioning one more time, then it's off to rehearse the graduation parade. You're out of the woods now. Congratulations. However, OCS has you for a bit longer. Thursday you'll also get Family Day orientation (a reminder not to act like an idiot when you see your girlfriend or boyfriend for the first time in ten weeks) and then it's off to Family Day at 1100. Enjoy it (no sarcasm this time.) This will be one of the proudest moments of your life. On Friday, you'll – surprise! Rehearse graduation one more time before actually performing the graduation parade. Afterward, you'll turn in your weapons at the armory, then head off to the museum for commissioning in the afternoon.

# Leadership

*"Speak softly and carry a big stick."*

-President Teddy Roosevelt

There isn't much we can teach you about leadership in this book that they won't teach better at OCS. Along with West Point, it is one of the finest leadership schools in the nation. However, we've got some pointers lined up for the things they *won't* tell you.

No surprise here, but leadership and the ability to lead is paramount at OCS. In fact, the ability to lead is 50% of your evaluation grade. Your potential as a leader in the Marine Corps will be evaluated through use of observation reports, leadership ratings, graded exams, peer evaluations, and other various practical applications.

## Leadership Billets

You will be given some form of a position of leadership at least once or twice. By the end of the sixth week, the candidates pretty much "run" the platoon with the Sergeant Instructors only watching, evaluating and offering pertinent advice (usually in the form of suggesting you are of illegitimate lineage or that you are mildly retarded. Usually both.)

Leadership billets are given for different reasons. You will have some people that are prior enlisted and it's not too big of deal for them, because they've done it before or seen it done. Usually, they will get selected for these billets early on, so pay close attention, because if they screw up, you could be next. For others it will be because the instructors already targeted someone, because they don't think the candidate is qualified and want to force them out, so they set them up for extreme failure. Usually, it's somewhere in the middle.  They aren't sure about a candidate one way or the other and want to give them another opportunity to prove themselves.  If you are a very strong candidate, they may just want to push you a little harder to see how capable you really are.

Another aspect of billets is that the entire time you are at OCS, they are building a case against you.  If they decide to kick you out, and you have to go to a review board, you will have a file an inch thick of everything you did wrong and all the essays you had to write.  A lot of it might be bullshit – and everyone knows that.  However, by giving you multiple leadership billets, you will have been evaluated by different people, so you really don't have any defense.  You can't say "well, so-and-so just had it out for me because they hated me for no good reason. I didn't get a fair chance."  Everyone gets a fair chance.  That's important to know – *everyone* gets a fair chance.

You will notice good people manage to fall between the cracks.  They might only get a very minor leadership billet once or twice, but otherwise get left alone by the Sergeant Instructors. This can be for any of the aforementioned reasons, but often they are just in the middle of the pack and don't stand out either way.  This is the case for probably about 50% of people, simply for the fact that there are only three instructors for 50-60 candidates, so it stands to reason that the very top and very bottom will get the "special" attention.

**General Leadership**

Leadership counts for 50% of your scores at OCS, and your chances to prove your ability will come in a few different forms.  Most notable of those are the Small Unit Leadership Exams I and II.  In both, you'll be divided into a small group (a squad) and each person will have to take their turn leading the others through some make-believe scenario such as "you have to move this heavy box of ammo across this body of water, but you can't touch the water." In each case, 10% of your score is about whether you accomplish the goal, and 90% is how you handle yourself and "lead". It actually doesn't have anything to do with anything in real life and how things would actually go, because you know you are being watched and you have to do certain things in certain ways. In short, it's not realistic and the results of it are not realistic, but if you can't even do this then you probably aren't cut out for Marine Corps leadership. Just take good notes as the situation is explained to you, then tell it to your team, set up security (very important, don't forget about any imaginary enemies in the area), give clear/concise directions to team, direct them professionally (don't ask them,) and etc. and so forth.

## The Dreaded Blue Falcon

Don't be a blue falcon (this is military code for "buddy fucker") and try to overtake a leadership role when it is someone else's turn. Even if the other guy is royally screwing up, don't just jump in and try to make yourself look good. Try this: "Hey, candidate Schmuckatelli, I just saw this rope over here, do you want me to do something with it?" Ask them like you need directions. In the real world, you wouldn't overstep your boundaries with someone in a leadership position over you, so don't do it here. You are not being graded at the time – the "leader" is – and it will do nothing but hurt the other guy and give you a bad reputation among your own platoon. This will hurt you big time in peer reviews. Simply let that person flail and struggle and fail on their own. You don't have to jump in and "save them" or try to take over. If they truly suck that bad, they'll get low enough scores and get kicked out.

# Academics

*"The relation between officers and men should in no sense be that of superior and inferior nor that of master and servant, but rather that of teacher and scholar... to the extent that officers, especially commanding officers, are responsible for the physical, mental, and moral welfare, as well as the discipline and military training of the young men under their command."*

—MajGen John A. Lejeune, 13th CMC: Marine Corps Manual, 1929

Someday, you are going to command troops, and you are going to need to teach them everything they need to know to survive and win battles, so that they can return to their families safe. That is your sacred obligation to your Marines, and the time for you to start taking that seriously is right now.

Academics accounts for 25% of your evaluation grade at OCS. There is a lot you will be taught, but there is no excuse for not being at least 90% proficient in everything before shipping. There is no reason to spend hours studying at night when you should be sleeping. We'll cover what you should know by heart and have committed to memory for life, and that which you just need a cursory knowledge of (although memorizing now is a good idea).

## MEMORIZE ALL OF THE FOLLOWING

You should have the following items memorized so well, you will remember then in twenty years – because you will be teaching it to a lot of junior Marines. You'll be tested on your knowledge of these things under pressure, so make sure you know them well before you leave for OCS.

## Leadership Traits

The mnemonic device for the Leadership Traits is:
JJ DID TIE BUCKLE.

JUSTICE
JUDGEMENT
DECISIVENESS
INTEGRITY
DEPENDABILITY
TACT
INITIATIVE
ENTHUSIASM
BEARING
UNSELFISHNESS
COURAGE (PHYSICAL & MORAL)
KNOWLEDGE
LOYALTY
ENDURANCE

## Leadership Principles

1.  Know yourself and seek self-improvement.
2.  Be technically and tactically proficient.
3.  Seek responsibility and take responsibility for your actions.
4.  Make sound and timely decisions.
5.  Set the example.
6.  Know your men and look out for their welfare.
7.  Keep your men informed.
8.  Develop a sense of responsibility in your subordinates.
9.  Ensure that the task is understood supervised and accomplished.
10. Train your men as a team.
11. Employ your unit in accordance with its capabilities.

## General Orders of the Guard

1. To take charge of this post and all government property in view.

2. To walk my post in a military manner, keeping always on the alert, observing everything that takes place within sight or hearing.

3. To report all violations of orders I am instructed to enforce.

4. To repeat all calls from posts more distant from the guardhouse than my own.

5. To quit my post only when properly relieved.

6. To receive, obey, and pass on to the sentry who relieves me: all orders from the commanding officer, officer of the day, and officers and non-commissioned officers of the guard only.

7. To talk to no one except in the line of duty.

8. To give the alarm in case of fire or disorder.

9. To call the corporal of the guard in any case not covered by instructions.

10. To salute, all officers and all colors and standards not cased.

11. To be especially watchful at night, and during the time for challenging, to challenge all persons on or near my post, and to allow no one to pass without proper authority.

## Code of Conduct

ARTICLE I.
I am an American, fighting in the forces which guard my country and our way of life. I am prepared to give my life in their defense.

ARTICLE II.
I will never surrender of my own free will. If in command, I will never surrender the members of my command while they still have the means to resist.

ARTICLE III.
If I am captured, I will continue to resist by all means available. I will make every effort to escape and aid others to escape. I will accept neither parole nor special favors from the enemy.

ARTICLE IV.
If I become a prisoner of war, I will keep faith with my fellow prisoners. I will give no information or take part in any action which might be harmful to my comrades. If I am senior, I will take command. If not, I will obey the lawful orders of those appointed over me and will back them up in every way.

ARTICLE V.
When questioned, should I become a prisoner of war, I am required to give name, rank, service number, and date of birth. I will evade answering further questions to the utmost of my ability. I will make no oral or written statements disloyal to my country and its allies or harmful to their cause.

ARTICLE VI.
I will never forget that I am an American, fighting for freedom, responsible for my actions, and dedicated to the principles which made my country free. I will trust in my God and in the United States of America.

## Rank Structure

Know Marine Corps ranks by heart before you leave.  There is no excuse for not being able to immediately recognize and properly address any officer or NCO.  You should also be familiar with Navy rank structure, although you don't need to have that as well memorized (you will pick it up over time.)  Army rank structure tracks closely with the Marines (Marines have different names for certain kinds of E-4s, all E-7s and certain kinds of E-9s) and if any Marine has ever figured out the Air Force's rank structure, please ask them to write the authors of this book and have them explain it to us.  Here is the Marine Corps rank structure:

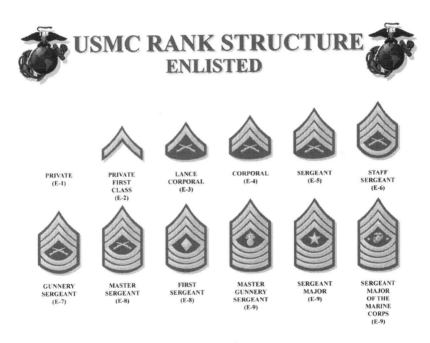

59

You can find all Marine Corps ranks and their insignia at marines.mil if you ever need a refresher.

## The M-16A4 Service Rifle

There is a very slight chance your unit will still use the M16-A2 at OCS (but almost definitely not at TBS.) If you are using the A2, the only difference is that it's a little lighter and it's more difficult to attach things to the barrel (which you probably won't do at OCS.) Other than that, all of the following information still applies:

*Nomenclature:* The M-16A4 Service Rifle is a lightweight, magazine-fed, gas-operated, air-cooled, shoulder-fired weapon. The acronym to remember this is LM-GAS.

*Three Main Groups:* The M-16A4 is made up of three groups of parts: The Upper Receiver Group, the Lower Receiver Group and the Bolt Carrier Group. You'll learn more about these in detail at OCS, but for now, make sure to have this memorized.

*Firing modes:* The M-16A4 has two firing modes: Semiautomatic, in which depressing the trigger will fire a single round, and automatic, in which depressing the trigger will fire a three-round burst. A quick note for you: You are training to join the United States Marine Corps, and we never waste ammunition. We have had a worldwide reputation for being the finest marksmen in the world for over two hundred years, and one of our mottos is "one shot, one kill." Unless you encounter the very rare circumstance in which you are instructed to set your rifle to "burst," you will always shoot in the semiautomatic firing mode. One bullet in an enemy's center mass is better than three to his shoulder, leg and ankle. Take pride in accuracy and deadly precision.

*Weight without sling, magazine and bayonet:* 7.5 pounds

*Weight with sling, 30-round magazine and bayonet:* 9.4 pounds

*Maximum range:* 3,534 meters

*Maximum effective range:* 800 meters for an area target and 550 meters for a point target.

*Maximum effective rate of fire:* 45 rounds per minute in semiautomatic, 90 rounds per minute in automatic.

The only authorized fluid for cleaning and lubricating the M16 – or any military rifle – is called CLP, which stands for cleaner, lubricant, protectant.

**BE FAMILIAR WITH THE FOLLOWING:**

You won't yet have learned how to implement all of this information, but you should have at least a cursory knowledge before shipping. You will be expected to actually use some of this stuff at OCS.

**Basic Marine Corps Terminology**

You will learn all of this at OCS, but it is a good idea to get ahead of the curve and learn some Marine Corps (and naval) terminology before you head off:

*Use proper rank for everyone you meet until you get to know them:* You may learn that there are nicknames for ranks. But you should never call a Marine by anything other than his or her full rank until you have worked with them for a while (unless they introduce themselves as such or give you explicit permission to call them by their rank's nickname.) These are terms of endearment, and like everything else in the Marine Corps, the permission to use them with each individual must always be earned . Another note: In the Army, anyone from a Sergeant to a Master Sergeant may be called "Sergeant" or "Sarge" (depending on circumstances.) We do not do this in the Marine Corps: A Staff Sergeant is always called "Staff Sergeant." And if you ever call a Sergeant of Marines by the name of "Sarge," he will lose his fucking mind, and have a right to do so, so don't tempt fate.

Here is a quick rundown of common nicknames for ranks, and a little context to help you know when nicknames are okay and when they are not:

*PFC:* The acronym for Private First Class. This is a perfectly acceptable acronym for Privates First Class – they will respond to it and use it to refer to themselves and others.

*Lance Coconut, Lance Criminal, Lance Colonel:* These are all nicknames for Lance Corporals. It is okay for them to refer to each other with these terms, but you shouldn't. Use their full ranks. Lance Corporal is one of the most difficult ranks for an enlisted Marine – when they have a lot of work and a lot of responsibility, but not much rank or respect, and you showing them respect means a lot to them.

*Gunny:* This is a shortened version of "Gunnery Sergeant." Many Gunnery Sergeants prefer the term "Gunny," but you can show your respect by waiting to be given permission to use the nickname, or until you have worked closely with them for some time.

*Top:* This is a nickname for Master Sergeants. Like "Gunny," wait until you have permission or a good working relationship to begin referring to Marines in this manner.

*Master Guns:* This is a nickname for Master Gunnery Sergeants. Like "Gunny," wait until you have permission or a good working relationship to begin referring to Marines in this manner.

*Lieutenant:* It is generally considered acceptable to refer to both $2^{nd}$ and $1^{st}$ Lieutenants simply as "Lieutenant."

*LT:* Lieutenants are sometimes called "LT" indirectly, but it is never appropriate to directly address them as such.

*Major:* A Captain may sometimes be referred to as "Major" if aboard a ship where a Navy Captain is present. There can only be one Captain on a ship, so the Marine Corps Captain is referred to as one rank higher.

*Skipper:* This is a nickname for Captains and above who are in command billets. It is appropriate to refer to "the Skipper" indirectly but generally inappropriate to address an officer as such (unless you outrank them, which you won't – for a while.)

*Colonel:* It is generally considered acceptable to refer to both Lieutenant Colonels and Colonels simply as "Colonel."

*Light Bird/Full Bird.* Lieutenant Colonels are sometimes called "Light Birds" and Colonels are sometimes called "Full Birds." It is never acceptable to address an officer with these titles, though they may be referred to in this manner.

**Other Terms to Know Before You Leave:**

*782 Gear or "Deuce" Gear*" Standard-issue gear, such as your pack, load-bearing vest, first-aid kit and everything else that will go along with you on a hump. It gets its name from the Marine Corps Form 782, which Marines used to have to sign to take responsibility for their gear.

*"As you were."* This means disregard the last order.

*Aye-aye.* This means "I understand the order and will carry it out." When answering a question in the affirmative, the appropriate response is, "Yes, sir." When acknowledging an order, the appropriate response is "aye-aye, sir." Do not be lazy and abbreviate this to a single "aye, sir." Someone will call you out on it.

*BCG's*: Known as "Birth Control Glasses", these Basic Combat Glasses will be issued to all candidates who normally wear glasses or contacts. You may NOT wear contacts while training at OCS. Trust us, you won't have an opportunity to fix your contacts when muddy water gets in it.

*Billet:* This is a task or title given to Marines that is separate from rank. A "platoon guide" is someone at the head of a platoon, a "squad leader" leads a squad, and a "platoon sergeant" is the top sergeant in a platoon, even though there may be other sergeants. Billets are usually commensurate with rank – for instance, a First Sergeant will most often act as "Company First Sergeant," although if there are no First Sergeants available, a Marine of a lower rank with the ability to perform may be selected to fill that billet.

*Boot:* Someone who is brand new to the Marine Corps (or brand new to a rank or billet.) For instance, a Staff Sergeant who has just been promoted to Gunnery Sergeant may be referred to by his *enlisted* superiors as a "boot Gunny." You are an officer, so don't ever call a Marine a "boot Gunny" until you're at least a Major – but even then, it's never really appropriate for an officer to refer to an enlisted Marine as "boot" anything, so know the term, but don't use it.

*Boots and Utes.* This is a slang term for exercising in camouflage utilities with the blouse removed. This is the uniform for most martial arts training and the Combat Fitness Test.

*Brig.* This is a term for military prison.

*Charlies.* A term for the service "C" uniform.

*CMC* – an acronym for "Commandant of the Marine Corps." Often written, rarely verbalized.

*Corframs* – dress shoes worn with the service and dress uniforms.

*Cover* – a term for the hats worn in uniform.

*Deck*: On a ship, the floor is known as the "deck." In the Marine Corps, all floors are known as the deck, no matter whether you are at sea or not.

*Firewatch* – a term for sentries watching a specific non-combat area. Comes from naval days when a guard would be posted to watch for fires on the ship. You will stand a lot of firewatch at OCS.

*Go-fasters* – a term for tennis shoes used in OCS, but not outside.

*Head*: This is the naval terminology for the restroom, so named because in olden days, sailors and Marines used to relieve themselves into the ocean from the head of the ship.

*Inkstick* – a term for a pen.

*Leadstick* – a term for a pencil.

*OFP* – an acronym meaning "own fucking program." This is a Marine who essentially does what he or she wants without leadership getting involved (or without leadership's knowledge.) Usually a pejorative.

*PCP* – a pejorative acronym for BCP, the Body Conditioning Platoon. Also called "Pork Chop Platoon."

*Salty* – means "experienced."

*Squadbay* – the place you will live in OCS. A barracks with a large open rooms and lined-up bunks, and a shared head.

*Troop* – this is a major insult to Marines unless used to refer to a group of them as "troops." Never call an individual Marine a "troop."

*Unq* – "unqualified." Usually in conjunction with someone who fails their marksmanship test on the range.

*Whiskey Locker* – the supply locker or closet

*Whiskey Tango Foxtrot* – the phonetic alphabetical spelling of "WTF" or "What the Fuck"

## BAMCIS

This is the acronym for the troop leadership process.

B = Begin Planning

A = Arrange for Reconnaissance and Coordination

M = Make Reconnaissance

C = Complete the Planning

I = Issue the Order

S = Supervise

## METT- T

This is the acronym used to estimate a situation in combat.

M = Mission

E = Enemy

T = Troops and Fire Support

T = Terrain and Weather

T = Time

## SALUTE

The acronym used to organize information about the enemy.

S = Size

A = Activity

L = Location

U = Unit

T = Time

E = Equipment

**OSMEAC**

The acronym used to remember the structure of a five-paragraph order. This is sometimes written as SMEAC.

O = Orientation
S = Situation
M = Mission
E = Execution
A = Administration and Logistics
C = Command and Signal

**Basic History of the Marine Corps**

You'll eventually need to learn and remember much more than this, but this is the very basic, but essential information you should have committed to memory before shipping. You'll learn more and in much more detail in the classroom.

- General Jacob Zeilin adopted the Marine Corps Emblem, the Eagle, Globe and Anchor, in 1868. The Globe depicts the western hemisphere, to show the global service and reach of the Marine Corps. The eagle symbolizes America, and the anchor with rope wrapped around it (the "fouled" anchor) symbolizes the Marine Corps' naval traditions and roots.

- The Marine Corps Motto is *Semper Fidelis*, which means Always Faithful. The motto was adopted in 1883.

- The Continental Congress founded the Marine Corps on 10 November 1775. The 13th Commandant of the Marine Corps, Major General John A. Lejeune, established the birthday celebration.

- Two Marines have received *two* Medals of Honor, Gunnery Sergeant Dan Daly and Major General Smedley Butler. For instant motivation, go read these guys' stories. If you want to explode with moto, go read about Gunnery Sergeant John Basilone's fighting in the Pacific.

- Major General Lewis "Chesty" Puller received 5 navy crosses.

- The Mameluke Sword was awarded to Lieutenant Pressley O'Bannon after the battle of Tripoli. It is the oldest weapon still in use in the military today.

- Opha Mae Johnson was the first female marine.

- A. A. Cunningham was the first marine aviator.

- The term "leatherneck" was given to early Marines because of the leather piece they wore around their neck to prevent an enemy's saber strike. The collar on the present day dress coat is raised and stiff to connect us to Marine Corps history.

## REQUIRED READING

A lot of people turn their nose up at the Commandant's Reading List, because it's "optional," (technically it's required, but hardly any Marines actually complete the reading for their rank.) They think the reading list is for nerds and "motards" (a pejorative for those Marines "uncool" enough to be motivated, proud to be a Marine, and not yet a jaded, cynical asshole.)

Be a nerdy motard. Read every book on the Commandant's Reading List for candidates before you go.

BONUS:  In the Marine Corps, there is a saying that goes, "Act like the next rank up."  The next rank up from Candidate is Second Lieutenant.  If you want to kick some serious ass and show everyone you mean business when you get to OCS, roll through the Commandant's Reading List for Second Lieutenants, too.

**The Commandant's Reading List for All Marines**

- *A Message to Garcia* by Elbert Hubbard.  Find it free online http://www.archive.org/stream/cu31924031017589#page /n5/mode/2up

- *MCWP 6-11: Leading Marines*.  Find it free online http://www.marines.mil/Portals/59/Publications/MCWP% 206-11%20Leading%20Marine.pdf

- *The Warrior Ethos* by Steven Pressfield.

- *MCDP-1: Warfighting.*  Find it free online http://www.marines.mil/Portals/59/Publications/MCDP%2 01%20Warfighting.pdf

- *MCRP 6-11D: Sustaining the Transformation.*  Find it free online http://community.marines.mil/news/publications/Docume nts/MCRP%206- 11D%20Sustaining%20the%20Transformation.pdf .

**The Commandant's Reading List for Entry-Level Officers**

- *Battle Cry* by Leon Uris.
- *Corps Values* by Zell Miller.
- *I'm Staying with My Boys* by Jerry Cutter.
- *Making the Corps* by Thomas Ricks.
- *My Men are Heroes* by Nathaniel Helms.
- *The Killer Angels* by Michael Shaara.


**The Commandant's Reading List for Second Lieutenants**

- *Battle Leadership* by Adolf Von Schell.
- *Gates of Fire* by Steven Pressfield.
- *Marine! The Life of Chesty Puller* by Burke Davis.
- *Matterhorn* by Karl Marlantes.
- *The Art of War* by Sun Tzu.
- *The Defence of Duffer's Drift* by Ernest Swinton.
- *Forgotten Soldier* by Guy Sajer.
- *The Last Stand of Fox Company* by Bob Drury and Tom Clavin.
- *The Marines of Montford Point* by Melton McLaurin.
- *The United States Constitution.*
- *With the Old Breed* by E.B. Sledge.

# Physical Fitness

*"You cannot exaggerate about the Marines. They are convinced to the point of arrogance that they are the most ferocious fighters on earth – and the amusing thing about it is that they are."*

-Father Kevin Keaney, 1st Marine Division Chaplain

Hey, preacher: You're damn skippy. But Marines can't be ferocious if we're not in magnificent physical condition, and you can't even become a Marine if you aren't in tip top shape. Don't rely on the grueling PT at OCS to get you strong – get strong first, and leave everyone else in the dust.

We will furnish you with a workout plan to make sure you have no problems at OCS, but first here is a little context:

**Overview**

It's been said that Quantico was put on earth for the sole purpose of training officer candidates. It is indeed a demanding climate and terrain and requires specific physical training before arriving. One aspect that cannot be trained for, but needs to be appreciated, is the severe humidity. Quantico is a swamp. A giant swamp. When you go for a run into the woods, you can feel a wall of humidity – sixty seconds into your run, you will be soaked from head to toe. This humidity, along with the sticky and muddy trails that accompany it, will make running more difficult than running on pavement or concrete. The point is, you need to be capable of performing at a high level at OCS, so you need to train in similar conditions. There is a reason the instructors get there early and train almost daily: they need to get acclimated so they don't struggle like the candidates likely will. Physical Training accounts for 25% of your evaluation scores at OCS.

**The Physical Fitness Test**

This test is a major component of your promotions – so it is incredibly important to max out your score. The test consists of crunches, pull-ups and a three-mile run. To max your score, you will need 100 crunches in two minutes, 20 pull-ups in a single set, and the ability to run three miles in eighteen minutes or less. If you follow this program, you will be able to knock this test out with no problems. Some people, however, struggle with their core strength. There are no abdominal exercises in this program, because strengthening your other muscles gives your core a solid workout. If you find that you are not able to do 100 crunches in two minutes, add in three max sets every morning, along with your morning push-ups (more on this in a moment.)

**The Combat Fitness Test (CFT)**

This is a relatively new test introduced a few years ago that favors strength over endurance. The training in this book will help you ace the CFT – which is also an important component of your promotion ability.

The test is made up of three parts, and all perfect score figures assume that you are between the ages of 18 and 26:

1. Run 880 yards in camouflage utilities (minus the blouse.) This means in boots. In order to get a perfect score, you will need to run it under a time of 2:45.
2. Lift a 30-pound ammo box over your head dozens of times. To get a perfect score, you will need to lift the ammo box 91 times.
3. Run the Maneuver Under Fire course. This consists of a series of sprints, crawls, grenade tosses, ammo-box carrying and fireman's carries. A fireman's carry is one in which you will need to lift a fellow candidate of a similar weight up and run a few hundred meters with them on

your back.  This is *very difficult*, especially if you are a larger or heavier candidate.  However, the program in this book takes into account the rigors of the Maneuver Under Fire, and exercises like the Deadlift and Squat will more than prepare you for this undertaking.  Check the Addenda for a great video of Marines running the CFT.

A final note about the CFT:  It is just as important to be a good partner as a strong partner.  When you take your turn being lifted, don't drag your heels during the buddy drag (slide along your soles) and support your fellow candidate's stance by placing your hand on his or her lower back while they are fireman's carrying you.  The instructors at OCS should give you a full instructional period on these measures, but sometimes it gets lost in the frenetic pace of training, so now you know.  Don't be a Blue Falcon!

**Running**

Never run on a treadmill when training for OCS.  The moving belt robs your calves of the opportunity to push off and strengthen your tendons and ligaments – not to mention the muscle itself.  Whenever possible, get out and run on soft grass, sand or mud.  Screw your shoes up.  You can afford new ones once you're a lieutenant.

There is one exception to the rule about treadmills:  If you live in Flatsville, USA and there are no hills to run, incorporate two or three visits to the gym *per week* to run at an incline on a treadmill.  You will run hills at OCS, and eventually you will face a hill called "Da Nang."  This giant, steep, muddy monster of a hill will destroy you if you don't train.

When you are running, don't just shoot for long marathons that will build your endurance.  You need to run sprints.  In the program included with this book, we'll incorporate sprints along with Fartlek runs.  For those of your that don't know, Fartlek is pronounced

75

"fart-lick" (get your snickers out now) and these runs consist of running for about the length of a city block, then dropping and doing a set of thirty reps on a given calisthenics exercise, such as push-ups, crunches or squats.  Fartlek is also known as HIIT, or High Intensity Interval Training.

## Strength Training

PT is not all running at OCS, although you can count on running *a lot.* Workouts extend far beyond what you do on the Physical Fitness Test (PFT) so do not train exclusively for the PFT. You will need to work on your upper body strength. This is a major weak point for male and females alike, but especially females. You will be surprised how much you end up doing upper body workouts during PT at OCS. Also, remember that you will not lift weights at OCS, so don't waste your time in front of the mirror at the gym getting pretty. You need to lift some weights to build strength, but the bulk of our program is focused on building up your calisthenics endurance, because that is primarily what you will suffer in Quantico.

## Time to Workout

Try getting up early (4:30am) and working out. Don't eat a large meal beforehand – in fact, it's best to drink a protein shake before and after your run (never run on an empty stomach during training, even though you may have to in OCS.) You don't have to get up this early for the entire program, but starting a week or two before you ship off, get your body and brain used to waking up that early so it's not a shock to your system. However, that means going to bed at a reasonable hour, as well. It is extremely important to get adequate rest in the weeks prior to going to OCS. You need eight to nine hours of sleep a night – especially if you are training hard. Just like running a marathon, you don't go out and run twenty miles the day before the big event. Rest, pound water, and eat high quality, nutritious food.

## PT in Boots

Once a week, run with your boots on. Running in boots on pavement will hurt your ankles and/or give you shin splints and put you in a worse situation. If you don't live anywhere near nature, just run alongside the sidewalk – and if there is no grass or dirt alongside the sidewalks near you, get down to a track at a local high school or college. Most of the running you do at OCS will be muddy and wet, even in your go-fasters (this is the OCS word for tennis shoes), but you will have some PT days in boots and utilities, so get used to it now.

## Humps

Grab a backpack, fill it up with 50 lbs or so and go for a walk. Start with as many miles as you can manage, then try to get to where you can go 4-6 miles without stopping. Take a ten minute break to drink water, check your feet, change socks if needed, then do another 4-6 miles. In case we failed to sufficiently make the point earlier, your humps will not be over flat terrain at OCS.

## Avoiding Injury by Stretching

Stretch daily. 7 days a week. Flexibility is very often the difference between getting *hurt* and getting *injured*. You will be doing a lot of activities where flexibility can help you finish faster and easier. Stretch your upper body as well as your legs too.

If you do get shin splints while training, there is only one cure and that's RICE: rest, ice, compression, elevation. It sucks, but that's the only way to make it go away. Do not show up to OCS with shin-splints, or you won't be there too long.

## Upper Body

You'll need to be strong – and you will need to be able to do a lot of pull-ups. We'll cover the Armstrong method in the upcoming plan.

You will do more push-ups at OCS than at nearly any other point in your Marine Corps career. Push-ups are usually the Army's gig, so this is the only two-and-a-half-month period of your life where your chest will be so sore that you want to puke.  However, you should be able to do at least one hundred pushups without stopping.  You will do a *lot* of PT at OCS that requires upper body strength.  Often, the PT instructor will work you through pushup workouts; they will do it with you, but remember these guys can do about 10 billion pushups without breaking a sweat, and will push you hard.

### The Armstrong Method for Pull-Ups

Major Charles Armstrong developed a program to get you to twenty pull-ups, and it works.  It takes dedication, but if you stick with it, you will get there – and be one of the rare candidates that knocks out twenty pull-ups on the first day of OCS.  Here's how it works.

*Every Morning:*

Wake up and immediately perform the maximum number of push-ups you can.

Use the bathroom, then perform another maximum set of push-ups.

Shave, then perform another maximum set of push-ups.

*Monday Afternoon* (at least four hours after push-ups):

Five maximum sets of pull-ups with ninety seconds of rest in between each one.

*Tuesday Afternoon*

Pull-up Pyramid: Start with one rep, rest for ten seconds, then do two reps, rest for twenty seconds, then three, then rest for thirty seconds, and continue until you "miss a set." For example, if your next set was supposed to be seven, but you could only do four, you missed a set. Rest for one minute, and then do one more maximum set.

*Wednesday Afternoon*

Three training sets of overhand grip.

Three training sets of underhand grip.

A training set is different for everyone. Essentially, it's the number of pull-ups you can squeeze into each set and still finish the day's workout. *It is essential to finish every day's workout.* No wimping out – you are just cheating yourself.

If you can do ten pull-ups in a maximum set, your training set is probably right around one or two pull-ups per training set. Above 15, you are probably around three or four pull-ups.

*Thursday Afternoon*

Do as many training sets as you can muster, with sixty seconds of rest in between, until you can't even complete one pull-up.

*Friday Afternoon*

Look back over the week and determine which day was hardest. Repeat it today.

# Nine-Week Physical Training Program

Before you balk at a physical training program that is almost as long as OCS itself, take a little heart: The last week is mostly rest and recuperation as you prepare to ship off. Also, this program is designed for those folks who haven't worked out in a while – so if you are strong enough to load the weight on, *go all the way to the max.* If you can push your muscles to the point of failure, you will grow and get strong. If you stop when you're merely uncomfortable, you won't make any progress. One note: Always rest Saturdays and Sundays. It's okay to do a little light cardio on weekends – if you want to go play sports with friends or take a hike, that's okay, just be sure to go easy and only do it for recreational purposes, not training. Your body needs plenty of rest, especially as the program ramps up in later weeks, and your brain needs to take a break from focusing on OCS from time to time.

## Selecting Weight

When you start Week 5 and finally get into the gym to lift, you are aiming to build strength, not mass or endurance. That means selecting enough weight that you can lift the recommended number of repetitions and no more or less. If the weight is too light, you won't get strong. If it's too heavy, you won't be able to complete the reps and you might injure yourself.

## Practicing Good Form

If you want to be an overachiever, start going to the gym in Week 4 and practicing your form with light weight or no weight. It is extraordinarily important that you lift with good form, especially on exercises like rows, squats and deadlifts. Lifting with bad form not only greatly increases your chances of injury, it drastically reduces your strength gains. In the course of your Marine Corps career, you will see a lot of ego-driven powerlifting types in the gym bench pressing hundreds of pounds by kipping and compromising their form. Not only do they look stupid, they are stupid. With proper form, you can lift half the weight and get twice the results. Don't be stupid.

**Consider a Personal Trainer or Mentor**

Not everyone has the money to hire a personal trainer, but if you can afford a few sessions, it is more than worth your money just to get your form down correctly. Many gyms give you a complimentary session with a personal trainer when you first sign up, so take advantage of it. If you can't afford a personal trainer, ask a friend who lifts weights to help you out. If that fails, try a coach or someone else at your school (if you are in college) or even your OSO, if he or she has time to come down to the gym with you.

A little anecdote for you: One of the authors of this book was broke and hadn't been to college yet when he was preparing for enlisted boot camp. He walked up to a buff dude at the gym wearing a Marines shirt (this man turned out to be a Major in the Reserves) and said he was preparing to leave in two months. He and the Major swapped phone numbers and the Major gave him two sessions a week working on his form and strength conditioning all the way up until the day he left.

The moral of that story is that you have a mission to accomplish, and you need to get it done in any way possible. If you are too shy to walk up to a stranger, shell out the cash for a personal trainer. But never lift without proper form.

**Exercise Definitions**

If you have done any kind of strength training before – or you just didn't skip gym class in high school – you will recognize all of the exercises in this program and know how to perform them.

If for any reason you don't know what these exercises are, you are strongly encouraged to pair up with a personal trainer, experienced friend, coach, mentor or your OSO. For videos demonstrating each exercise (and its associated proper form) please visit the Exercise Library at bodybuilding.com.

Your program begins on the next page!

**Week One**

All of your strength training in Week One will come from the Armstrong Method.  For more detail, see the previous chapter.

| Day/Time | Cardio | Strength | Sets/Reps |
|---|---|---|---|
| Monday AM | Run (1 mile) | Push-ups | 3/maximum |
| Monday PM | Rest | Pull-ups | 5/maximum |
| Tuesday AM | Rest | Push-ups | 3/maximum |
| Tuesday PM | Rest | Pull-ups | Pyramid |
| Wednesday AM | Run (1.5 miles) | Push-ups | 3/maximum |
| Wednesday PM | Rest | Pull-ups | 6/training |
| Thursday AM | Rest | Push-ups | 3/maximum |
| Thursday PM | Rest | Pull-ups | maximum/training |
| Friday AM | Run (2 miles) | Push-ups | 3/maximum |
| Friday PM | Rest | Pull-ups | repeat hardest day |

## Week Two

We're still on the Armstrong Method for strength training.

| Day/Time | Cardio | Strength | Sets/Reps |
|---|---|---|---|
| Monday AM | Run (2 miles) | Push-ups | 3/maximum |
| Monday PM | Rest | Pull-ups | 5/maximum |
| Tuesday AM | Rest | Push-ups | 3/maximum |
| Tuesday PM | Rest | Pull-ups | Pyramid |
| Wednesday AM | Run (2 miles) | Push-ups | 3/maximum |
| Wednesday PM | Rest | Pull-ups | 6/training |
| Thursday AM | Rest | Push-ups | 3/maximum |
| Thursday PM | Rest | Pull-ups | maximum/training |
| Friday AM | Run (3 miles) | Push-ups | 3/maximum |
| Friday PM | Rest | Pull-ups | repeat hardest day |

## Week Three

Time to start ramping up the runs – but we're still on the Armstrong Method, and will be until Week Five.

| Day/Time | Cardio | Strength | Sets/Reps |
|----------|--------|----------|-----------|
| Monday AM | Hill Run (2 miles) | Push-ups | 3/maximum |
| Monday PM | Rest | Pull-ups | 5/maximum |
| Tuesday AM | Rest | Push-ups | 3/maximum |
| Tuesday PM | Rest | Pull-ups | Pyramid |
| Wednesday AM | Fartlek Run, 2 miles (with sprint intervals – 25m sprints every 150m) | Push-ups | 3/maximum |
| Wednesday PM | Rest | Pull-ups | 6/training |
| Thursday AM | Rest | Push-ups | 3/maximum |
| Thursday PM | Rest | Pull-ups | maximum/training |
| Friday AM | Run (4 miles) | Push-ups | 3/maximum |
| Friday PM | Rest | Pull-ups | repeat hardest day |

**Week Four**

We'll take a break from running most of the week. You should be seeing serious gains in your pull-ups by now.

| Day/Time | Cardio | Strength | Sets/Reps |
|----------|--------|----------|-----------|
| Monday AM | Hike (50 lbs, 2 miles) | Push-ups | 3/maximum |
| Monday PM | Rest | Pull-ups | 5/maximum |
| Tuesday AM | Rest | Push-ups | 3/maximum |
| Tuesday PM | Rest | Pull-ups | Pyramid |
| Wednesday AM | Hike (50 lbs, 4 miles) | Push-ups | 3/maximum |
| Wednesday PM | Rest | Pull-ups | 6/training |
| Thursday AM | Rest | Push-ups | 3/maximum |
| Thursday PM | Rest | Pull-ups | maximum/training |
| Friday AM | Run (5 miles) | Push-ups | 3/maximum |
| Friday PM | Rest | Pull-ups | repeat hardest day |

## Week Five

Now things get interesting.  We'll start running and hiking four times a week and start adding dedicated weightlifting to the Armstrong Method.  Time to get strong.

| Day/Time | Cardio | Strength | Sets/Reps |
|---|---|---|---|
| Monday AM | Run (5 miles) | Push-ups | 3/maximum |
| Monday PM | Rest | Pull-ups | 5/maximum |
| | Rest | Bench Press | 5/8 |
| | Rest | Bodyweight Dips | 5/maximum |
| Tuesday AM | Hike (50 lbs, 5 miles) | Push-ups | 3/maximum |
| Tuesday PM | Rest | Pull-ups | Pyramid |
| | | Lat Pulldowns | 5/8 |
| | | Rows | 5/8 |
| | | Bicep Curls | 5/8 |
| Wednesday AM | Rest | Push-ups | 3/maximum |
| Wednesday PM | Rest | Pull-ups | 6/training |
| | | Military Press | 5/8 |
| Thursday AM | Fartlek Run, 3 miles (50m sprints every 200m) | Push-ups | 3/maximum |
| Thursday PM | Rest | Pull-ups | maximum/training |
| Friday AM | Hill Run (4 miles) | Push-ups | 3/maximum |
| Friday PM | Rest | Pull-ups | repeat hardest day |
| | | Squats | 5/8 |
| | | Deadlifts | 5/8 |
| | | Leg Extensions | 5/8 |
| | | Hamstring Curls | 5/7 |

## Week Six

The same split as last week, but a lower amount of reps on the weight training (and you should use a higher weight.)

| Day/Time | Cardio | Strength | Sets/Reps |
|---|---|---|---|
| Monday AM | Run (6 miles) | Push-ups | 3/maximum |
| Monday PM | Rest | Pull-ups | 5/maximum |
| | Rest | Bench Press | 5/7 |
| | Rest | Weighted Dips | 5/7 |
| Tuesday AM | Hike (50 lbs, 6 miles) | Push-ups | 3/maximum |
| Tuesday PM | Rest | Pull-ups | Pyramid |
| | | Lat Pulldowns | 5/7 |
| | | Rows | 5/7 |
| | | Bicep Curls | 5/7 |
| Wednesday AM | Rest | Push-ups | 3/maximum |
| Wednesday PM | Rest | Pull-ups | 6/training |
| | | Military Press | 5/7 |
| Thursday AM | Fartlek Run, 4 miles (50m sprints every 200m) | Push-ups | 3/maximum |
| Thursday PM | Rest | Pull-ups | maximum/training |
| Friday AM | Hill Run (5 miles) | Push-ups | 3/maximum |
| Friday PM | Rest | Pull-ups | repeat hardest day |
| | | Squats | 5/7 |
| | | Deadlifts | 5/7 |
| | | Leg Extensions | 5/7 |
| | | Hamstring Curls | 5/7 |

**Week Seven**

You recognize the split by now, except we're hiking on Wednesday this week. Additionally, we will shake things up this week and freak your body out so it doesn't get complacent and stop growing. Lose the Armstrong Method this week, make a massive endurance gain. Here we go.

| Day/Time | Cardio | Strength | Sets/Reps |
|---|---|---|---|
| Monday AM | Hike (50 lbs, 6 miles) | Bench Press | 5/15 |
| Monday PM | Rest | Bodyweight Dips | 5/15 |
| Tuesday AM | Hill Run (5 miles) | Lat Pulldowns | 5/15 |
| Tuesday PM | Rest | Rows | 5/15 |
| | | Bicep Curls | 5/15 |
| Wednesday AM | Hike (50 lbs, 6 miles) | Military Press | 5/15 |
| Wednesday PM | Rest | Rest | Rest |
| Thursday AM | Fartlek Run, 4 miles (with sprint intervals – 75m sprints every 250m) | Rest | Rest |
| Thursday PM | Rest | Squats | 5/15 |
| Friday AM | Hill Run (5 miles) | Deadlifts | 5/15 |
| Friday PM | Rest | Leg Extensions | 5/15 |
| | | Hamstring Curls | 5/15 |
| | | Squats | 5/15 |

**Week Eight**

The hardest week of them all. Leave absolutely nothing when you are working out and use the heaviest weights possible – this is the week you will make the most crucial gains in strength for OCS.

| Day/Time | Cardio | Strength | Sets/Reps |
|---|---|---|---|
| Monday AM | Run (7 miles) | Push-ups | 3/maximum |
| Monday PM | Rest | Pull-ups | 5/maximum |
| | Rest | Bench Press | 5/5 |
| | Rest | Weighted Dips | 5/5 |
| Tuesday AM | Hike (50 lbs, 7 miles) | Push-ups | 3/maximum |
| Tuesday PM | Rest | Pull-ups | Pyramid |
| | | Lat Pulldowns | 5/5 |
| | | Rows | 5/5 |
| | | Bicep Curls | 5/5 |
| Wednesday AM | Hike (50 lbs, 7 miles) | Push-ups | 3/maximum |
| Wednesday PM | Rest | Pull-ups | 6/training |
| | | Military Press | 5/5 |
| Thursday AM | Fartlek Run, 5 miles (75m sprints every 250m) | Push-ups | 3/maximum |
| Thursday PM | Rest | Pull-ups | maximum/training |
| Friday AM | Hill Run (6 miles) | Push-ups | 3/maximum |
| Friday PM | Rest | Pull-ups | repeat hardest day |
| | | Squats | 5/5 |
| | | Deadlifts | 5/5 |
| | | Leg Extensions | 5/5 |
| | | Hamstring Curls | 5/5 |

**Week Nine**

It's time to stop strength training immediately and give your muscles a week off to rest and grow. You will still run – but only three times this week, and not too far or hard. This week is all about getting the rest and recuperation you need before you leave for OCS.

| Day/Time | Cardio |
|---|---|
| Monday AM | Run (5 miles) |
| Monday PM | Rest |
| Tuesday AM | Rest |
| Tuesday PM | Rest |
| Wednesday AM | Fartlek Run, 5 miles (with sprint intervals – 75m sprints every 250m) |
| Wednesday PM | Rest |
| Thursday AM | Rest |
| Thursday PM | Rest |
| Friday AM | Hill Run (5 miles) |
| Friday PM | Rest |

If you got to the end of the program, reward yourself with a nice dinner out and some couch potato days – especially the weekend before you take off. Congratulations! You will be head and shoulders above the rest once you hit OCS.

# The Seven-Day Nutrition Program

This chapter is much simpler than the previous. What it essentially aims to do is give you the basics of good nutrition – especially while you are working out – and give you a framework within which to operate. Stick to this framework all nine weeks of the workout program, and you will grow strong.

Let's start with some general principles of nutrition.

1. *Build your meals around lean protein, vegetables and fruits.* It's okay to eat carbohydrates – in fact, you'll need them while on the workout program. But you should strive to make up the bulk of your meals with lean protein like poultry and fish, and complex carbs like fruits and veggies. Minimize your intake of refined carbohydrates, like white bread, potatoes and white rice, and try to make sure you balance the fats you eat between saturated animal fats and healthy monounsaturated and polyunsaturated fats, such as those found in nuts and olive oil.

2. *Eat more protein than anything else.* Calories are calories, but protein has the amino acids you need to build and strengthen muscle and half as many calories per gram as fat. You want to get strong before OCS, not blubbery.

3. *Avoid processed foods, fast food and eating out in general.* These foods are mostly filled with all kinds of nasty chemicals you don't need in your body, and also tend to be empty calories devoid of nutrition. Regardless of what restaurants you like, they are in the business of making things taste as amazing as possible – not the nutritional bottom line. So even supposedly "healthy" offerings can

97

have hundreds more calories than what you would prepare at home. Also, making food yourself saves you a bundle of money.

4. *Stay hydrated.* Oftentimes, when we feel hungry, that is our body telling us it wants water. We get a lot of our daily water intake from food, so our body sometimes confuses the signals between hunger and thirst. Before you eat a snack, drink a glass of water and wait ten minutes. If the hunger goes away, you just needed to hydrate.

5. *Plan ahead.* It's best to do as much cooking ahead as possible. Try to cook in large batches on Sunday and Wednesday evenings, so you spend as little time in the kitchen as possible on other days of the week when you are busy.

6. *Don't be too tough on yourself.* And now, to mildly contradict everything else we just wrote, take it easy on yourself. There is nothing wrong with cheating on your diet from time to time – it acts as a pressure release valve. If you have a small portion of your favorite fatty foods from time to time, it will prevent you from losing your willpower down the road and binging on a gallon of ice cream and a whole pizza.

**The Program**

This program was designed with an average male college student in mind. If you are female or are a male that is substantially smaller or larger than the average American male (5'8" and 175 lbs.) you likely have different caloric needs than the target audience of this program, and will need to seek out another nutritional resource. If you are between 5'6" and 6' and between 150 lbs. and 200 lbs., this program will work well for you.

We strongly recommend you follow a nutritional program that is right for your body.  You can find many excellent nutritional resources at the Nutrition Knowledge page at bodybuilding.com if this particular program is not right for your body size.

You should have some basic cooking skills in order to successfully execute this program.  You'll notice that your grocery bill will go up at first, but if you quit ordering pizza and guzzling beer, you'll make up the savings down the road.

**Monday**

| Meal | Recipe | Calories | Fat | Carbs | Protein |
|------|--------|----------|-----|-------|---------|
| Breakfast | 2 Eggs fried in 1tbsp. olive oil, 2 slices of bacon | 426 | 37 | 1 | 20 |
| Post-AM Workout | 2 scoops whey protein in 12 oz. of 2% milk | 483 | 17 | 32 | 72 |
| Lunch | 2 slices whole-wheat bread, 1 tbsp. mayonnaise, 1 can tuna, leaf of lettuce, sliced onions | 515 | 19 | 31 | 48 |
| Snack | 1 oz. roasted almonds and 3 oz. blueberries | 207 | 15 | 6 | 7 |
| Post-PM Workout | 2 scoops whey protein in 12 oz. of 2% milk | 483 | 17 | 32 | 72 |
| Dinner | 6 oz. baked chicken breast, 2 cups cooked broccoli | 339 | 7 | 7 | 58 |
| **Totals** | | 2453 | 112 | 109 | 277 |

## Tuesday

| Meal | Recipe | Calories | Fat | Carbs | Protein |
|------|--------|----------|-----|-------|---------|
| Breakfast | 2 Eggs fried in 1tbsp. olive oil, 2 slices of bacon | 426 | 37 | 1 | 20 |
| Post-AM Workout | 2 scoops whey protein in 12 oz. of 2% milk | 483 | 17 | 32 | 72 |
| Lunch | 2 slices whole-wheat bread, 1 tbsp. mayonnaise, 4 oz. ham, leaf of lettuce, sliced onions, sliced tomato (mustard optional) | 485 | 18 | 31 | 41 |
| Snack | 2 oz. beef jerky | 232 | 14 | 3 | 18 |
| Post-PM Workout | 2 scoops whey protein in 12 oz. of 2% milk | 483 | 17 | 32 | 72 |
| Dinner | 8 oz. baked tilapia, 1 cup green beans | 594 | 28 | 28 | 62 |
| **Totals** | | 2703 | 131 | 127 | 285 |

## Wednesday

| Meal | Recipe | Calories | Fat | Carbs | Protein |
|------|--------|----------|-----|-------|---------|
| Breakfast | 1 cup oatmeal, 1 tsp. brown sugar | 183 | 4 | 29 | 6 |
| Post-AM Workout | 2 scoops whey protein in 12 oz. of 2% milk | 483 | 17 | 32 | 72 |
| Lunch | 6 oz. baked chicken breast, 2 cups cooked broccoli | 339 | 7 | 7 | 58 |
| Snack | 2 oz. beef jerky | 232 | 14 | 3 | 18 |
| Post-PM Workout | 2 scoops whey protein in 12 oz. of 2% milk | 483 | 17 | 32 | 72 |
| Dinner | 6 oz. baked pork tenderloin, 1 cup cooked spinach | 319 | 9 | 3 | 53 |
| **Totals** | | 2039 | 68 | 106 | 279 |

## Thursday

| Meal | Recipe | Calories | Fat | Carbs | Protein |
|------|--------|----------|-----|-------|---------|
| Breakfast | 1 cup oatmeal, 1 tsp. brown sugar, 2 eggs fried in 1 tbsp. olive oil | 368 | 18 | 30 | 19 |
| Post-AM Workout | 2 scoops whey protein in 12 oz. of 2% milk | 483 | 17 | 32 | 72 |
| Lunch | 2 slices whole-wheat bread, 1 tbsp. mayonnaise, 4 oz. ham, leaf of lettuce, sliced onions, sliced tomato (mustard optional) | 485 | 18 | 31 | 41 |
| Snack | 1 oz. roasted almonds and 3 oz. blueberries | 207 | 15 | 6 | 7 |
| Post-PM Workout | 2 scoops whey protein in 12 oz. of 2% milk | 483 | 17 | 32 | 72 |
| Dinner | 6 oz. broiled sirloin steak, 1 cup cooked peas | 348 | 7 | 14 | 37 |
| **Totals** | | 2404 | 93 | 145 | 255 |

**Friday**

| Meal | Recipe | Calories | Fat | Carbs | Protein |
|---|---|---|---|---|---|
| Breakfast | 2 Eggs fried in 1tbsp. olive oil, 2 slices of bacon | 426 | 37 | 1 | 20 |
| Post-AM Workout | 2 scoops whey protein in 12 oz. of 2% milk | 483 | 17 | 32 | 72 |
| Lunch | 2 slices whole-wheat bread, 1 tbsp. mayonnaise, 1 can tuna, leaf of lettuce, sliced onions | 515 | 19 | 31 | 48 |
| Snack | 2 oz. beef jerky | 232 | 14 | 3 | 18 |
| Post-PM Workout | 2 scoops whey protein in 12 oz. of 2% milk | 483 | 17 | 32 | 72 |
| Dinner | 8 oz. baked tilapia, 1 cup green beans | 594 | 28 | 28 | 62 |
| **Totals** | | 2733 | 132 | 127 | 292 |

## Saturday

| Meal | Recipe | Calories | Fat | Carbs | Protein |
|------|--------|----------|-----|-------|---------|
| Breakfast | 2 cups oatmeal, 2 tsp. brown sugar | 366 | 8 | 58 | 12 |
| Snack | 2 oz. roasted almonds and 6 oz. blueberries | 414 | 30 | 12 | 14 |
| Lunch | 2 slices whole-wheat bread, 1 tbsp. mayonnaise, 4 oz. ham, leaf of lettuce, sliced onions, sliced tomato (mustard optional) | 485 | 18 | 31 | 41 |
| Snack | 2 oz. beef jerky | 232 | 14 | 3 | 18 |
| Dinner | 12 oz. baked pork tenderloin, 2 cups cooked spinach | 638 | 18 | 6 | 106 |
| **Totals** | | 2135 | 88 | 110 | 191 |

## Sunday

| Meal | Recipe | Calories | Fat | Carbs | Protein |
|------|--------|----------|-----|-------|---------|
| Breakfast | 2 cups oatmeal, 2 tsp. brown sugar | 366 | 8 | 58 | 12 |
| Snack | 2 oz. roasted almonds and 6 oz. blueberries | 414 | 30 | 12 | 14 |
| Lunch | 2 slices whole-wheat bread, 1 tbsp. mayonnaise, 4 oz. ham, leaf of lettuce, sliced onions, sliced tomato (mustard optional) | 485 | 18 | 31 | 41 |
| Snack | 2 oz. beef jerky | 232 | 14 | 3 | 18 |
| Dinner | 12 oz. baked pork tenderloin, 2 cups cooked spinach | 638 | 18 | 6 | 106 |
| **Totals** | | 2135 | 88 | 110 | 191 |

# Miscellaneous

*"I come in peace. I didn't bring artillery. But I'm pleading with you, with tears in my eyes: If you fuck with me, I'll kill you all."*

- General James "Mad Dog" Mattis

There wasn't anywhere else in the book to put that quote, and even though it's the second quote from General Mad Dog so far, it's so delicious and moto it had to go somewhere.

Everything else that didn't really belong elsewhere in the book – but that you need to know – winds up in this section, too. Study it well.

### Juniors and Seniors

If you have not yet graduated college – and are just in your junior year – you can sign up for a special program in which you attend OCS over two years, meaning you go for six weeks your junior year and six weeks your senior year. If you are thinking this is a good deal because you only have to go for six weeks at a time, think again. It's the worst possible choice.

Think about it: Once you have been at OCS for six weeks, you have the hang of things. If you are a senior, you only have to tough out the last month – the month in which you are more or less running the platoon, the Sergeant Instructors are much less hard on you, and the final two weeks of which are more or less motivational and administrative.

If you are a junior and decide to split things up, you will go through the hardest six weeks of OCS, then go home. You will live and study for another year without any military rank (and without any respect) – all the while dreading your return to what is, essentially, some of the hardest training you will ever undergo in the Marines – before having to go back and ramp back up into military mode.    A year in between training is a lot of time, too, and all sorts of things happen, including sports injuries, weight gain or major life events that could seriously change your mind about wanting to become an Officer of Marines.

If you are committed to becoming an Officer of Marines, it is best to wait until your senior year of college and go for the ten-week course.  Not only is it shorter overall, there is much less distraction and opportunities to fail in between summers.

### Hydration

This is a general piece of advice:  Stay hydrated at all times, before, during and after OCS.  In particular, you need to show up to OCS well hydrated.  That means drink *lots* of water every day for about two weeks prior to shipping.  Do not drink any soda, keep sports drinks to a bare minimum if at all (get your body used to just plain old water.)  Eat extra salt, and avoid alcohol altogether, as it will only dehydrate you.  Pounding a gallon or two of water the day before you go will not cut it.

### Electrolytes

When at OCS, put a little extra salt your food & eat a banana with every meal.  You will be losing countless electrolytes, and Gatorade (which you are not allowed to drink for at least a few weeks) will not cut it.  You cannot risk cramping up and failing an event you could have passed.  You will be peeing constantly with all the water you need to stay hydrated, so you have to replace the sodium, potassium and other electrolytes that you are losing.

**Breaking in your Boots**

Buy your boots now. Go to quanticoboot.com and buy one pair of boots – Bates is a good brand. When you buy your boots, you will probably have to send them back once or twice to fine-tune the right size you need, because they are oddly-sized and the fit changes a *lot* between different brands. Make sure the brand you choose has the EGA on the heel or they won't be allowed at OCS. Once you get your boots, fill them with a garden hose so they are soaked as much as possible, tie them on tight and practice running with them once a week. Don't run more often than that, or you will wear them out ahead of time. Do just enough to break them in right.

The reason you want to get your boots now is because you will get more boots when you get there and go thru uniform issue. However, this process (like everything else) is rushed and you have very little time to figure out what boots are right. Even if you do get it right, you have humps in your near future, not to mention miles and miles of drill on the parade deck, and that is NOT a good time to break them in. Blisters can end your OCS stint in a hurry – some guys' heels and toes look like hell after a couple of weeks, and they get sent home  because they missed too many evaluations due to the fact that their feet looked like hamburger.

**Take Care of Your Feet**

Get Gold-Bond foot powder from the PX and take care of your feet. Powder them every night before you sleep and every morning before you put your boots on. You will be running through some of the most God-forsaken swamp water imaginable and you *have* to take care of your feet afterwards.

### Take Care of Your Weapon

Learn to clean your rifle quickly and *very* well. You will earn a lot of respect and brownie points from the instructors if you maintain your weapon well. One of the authors, while at OCS, got high scores during a review because the only thing the instructors could say about his rifle was there "was a piece of grass stuck on the butt stock," which was there from the ground. He also said, "Overall, this weapon is perfect condition and well maintained. Mark that down for this candidate." He moved on without fully inspecting much else on me at all.

We would love to give you a full primer on the M-16 service weapon, but a soldier's relationship to his or her rifle is intrinsic. It is a kinesthetic bond you won't truly understand until it has been attached to you – a kind of extension of your body – for weeks or months on end. After OCS and TBS (and especially after a deployment) many Marines sleeping at home in their nice, cozy bed still wake up in a sweat grasping at the absence of the weight and shape of their rifle. Once it is a part of you, it never leaves.

The best preparation you can make is to do some solid research on the weapon before you take off. We'll give you some pointers to get started – that is, the stuff you won't be able to find anywhere else – but you can also find some more detailed resources in the Addenda.

That said, here is our advice for taking care of your weapon: The best general precept when cleaning your M-16 is to first get your weapon back to square one, meaning get off all the mud, grease, oil, etc. These M-16's are often so brutalized already from years of service at OCS, you don't have to baby them. Some people completely submerge their weapons in water and scrub the hell out of them. This is *fine*. If you are familiar with guns and are crying foul at the idea of getting your weapon wet, just wait for the Quigley. You ain't going to get that crap off with CLP.

The next step is to dry it meticulously because by getting it wet (which again, it was already wet from all the fun you had that day in the swamps) there is a risk of rust. Even a speck of rust or patina (thin layer of rust) is an automatic inspection fail. The Sergeant Instructors will be looking in extreme detail, such as the groove in the head of a flat-head screw in the butt-stock.

Finally, once it is dry and scrubbed as much as necessary, lube that baby up. Be generous with it, then be a little more generous. Get it into all the nooks and crannies, letting it really soak in. Finally, use a towel to get that excess oil off and keep going with a fresh towel as needed. You will have to figure out your own process, but if you follow this general guideline, you will get a cleaner weapon and only spend about half the time doing so.

**Weapon Security**

Weapon security is paramount to the point it is unrealistic. Once, they took some candidates' weapons that were not properly locked to their racks while they were listening to a presentation from the platoon CO. The ass-chewing that ensued was pretty incredible.

There were statements made about terrorists coming onto military bases to steal weapons, and obviously those candidates didn't care about terrorists getting our weapons. This is obviously horse-shit. Al Qaeda's big idea is to risk detection and sneak onto USMC bases (the people whose job it is to kill them) and steal the most beat-to-hell piece of crap M16 that has been so abused by years of existence at OCS, that it could very damn near fall apart any second? Sure.

Although "terrorists stealing rifles" is a bit of a stretch, there is logic behind tight weapon security. Regardless of why, if that weapon is not on your body, it better have a lock on it. Period. It doesn't matter if you are about to crap your pants, you have to risk changing your shorts so you can lock that weapon first. The only exception is when people are designated to stand there and watch them, which you will get to do during chow a few times.

### Required Knowledge

*Study, study, study.* The instructors ask questions like "name five leadership traits and tell me which one is most important, and why." Have an answer for them.

### Speak in Third-Person

Never refer to yourself as "I," "me" or refer to something as "mine." Always say "this candidate" or "this candidate's." Part of the training is subverting your normal language processes to break down your mental processes and keep you under stress.

### Peer Evaluations

You'll have to do peer evaluations, or as some might call them, "spear evaluations." It's a shitty part of OCS, but is something you'll have to do later on as an officer, when you make fitness reports for others under your command. The difference is that at OCS, you have to rank people. Now, some squads have candidates that are hard-charging and squared away. All of them deserve a 95 or higher, but somebody has to be last. On the flip side, there are other squads of complete trash-bags and their best guy isn't up to par with another squad's worst, but he'll get high rating. It averages out, but it's hardly fair. Embrace the suck.

You will undoubtedly run across situations where someone is ranked last by everyone in the early weeks, but later turns out to be a top candidate that is pulling others along. You will see the exact opposite, too. This often happens in the case of prior enlisted candidates who are extremely helpful at first because they know how to make their rack and have general military know-how, but later on turn out to be jackasses who are sick of getting yelled at by guys they normally work convivially with. It seems to go to one extreme or the other for prior enlisted types, in that they are either great or terrible to work with, and will either finish at the top of the class or get the boot early on.  Write us an e-mail once you graduate and tell us we're wrong.

**Females**

There are three things to mention for our female readers.  First: Female candidates drop very quickly – due to injuries, not the inability to perform the training.  This is not because females are substantially weaker (many, if not most, female candidates have better endurance than males, if less overall strength) but the physical training is designed by men and for the specific strengths of men.  Yes, this is extraordinarily sexist.  Unfortunately, the Marine Corps is the most hyper-masculine organization in the world – maybe outside of the Russian mafia – and they haven't caught up with modern sensibilities.

Second:  Pull-ups and the obstacle course require twitch strength in large muscle groups, core stability and other strengths that many men have by virtue of their sex, but most women have to train to gain.  The physical fitness regimen at OCS is poorly adapted for physiological differences in females; add on top of that the fact that young men who join the military were more likely to play sports, thus conditioning them for the huge amount of physical training – and women just get injured more often. The sad reality is that far more women drop before graduation than men.

The last thing to mention is not directed at females, but at males, regarding the female Marines you will encounter.  If you think the male instructors are bad, you better watch out.  Female instructors make sure you don't get any sexist ideas in your head – and they will get extra deep up your ass if you give them a reason to, because they have dealt with sexist bullshit from chauvinist male Marines throughout their entire careers.  Female Marines are Marines, plain and simple, and deserve all of the respect afforded to male Marines.  If anything, they deserve a little more, because they are succeeding in a military organization that is 94% male.

**The Silver Bullet**

For those who have heard of the mythical "Silver Bullet", yes, it is real, and yes, the Navy Corpsman will use it.  For those of you who are unfamiliar, the silver bullet is the thermometer they will use to check your core temperature should you pass out during PT (or any time.)  For those of you who are challenged in the realm of anatomical knowledge, your core temperature is checked in your rectum.  They put this thing in your ass.  Not kidding.

As much as you may dread this experience, there are a couple things to note here.  First, if you go during the summer, there will be multiple people who pass out from heat and over-exhaustion.  If you do, they paint a big yellow circle on the back of your PT shirts so the corpsmen can quickly ID those who have succumbed to the heat previously.  The reality is, there is no shame in having passed out because you literally pushed yourself until your body collapsed.  There is shame in trying to tell a corpsman "I'm about to pass out," however.  Why? Because if you really were "about to pass out", you wouldn't be communicating very well and you would be pretty spaced out.  If you can verbalize that you are feeling crappy, you are okay - so keep going.  If that proposition is more than you are willing to commit to, don't bother going to OCS.  Don't worry, the corpsmen will not let you die from the heat.

# Final Advice

*"We are proud to claim the title of United States Marines."*
                              The Marines' Hymn, author unknown

Making it through OCS is a serious accomplishment. If you make it, you will have proven that you have what it takes and you should be proud of yourself. However, the path to proving yourself is far from over. The fact is, you still haven't done a damn thing in the real world. The gold bars on your collar mean little or nothing to an enlisted Private First Class (PFC) or Lance Corporal who has made a couple combat deployments. You will be viewed as a spoiled college boy until you *prove* otherwise. Nothing in the Marines is given – it must be earned.

Never forget that no amount of training or knowledge can ever replace experience. As the joke goes "What's the difference between a PFC and a 2$^{nd}$ LT? The PFC has been promoted once."

Lean heavily on your NCOs and their experience. As an officer, you will be the one who has to make the final decision, but they can give you invaluable information from their experience to help you make said decision. Be professional and be the leader that your Marines deserve. Not everyone will end up in a combat MOS, but the Marines you lead are all willing to do whatever it takes and risk their life, trusting in your decisions and abilities, sometimes putting to the side what they think should be done. Let that sink in. A fellow human being is willing to let you decide something that could be life or death for them, trusting that you will do what is right. They are willing to put *their* future, *their* family, *their* hopes and dreams in *your* hands. Nothing in this book – and nothing about OCS – should frighten you more than that responsibility. Respect the responsibility, respect your rank, respect your troops and respect yourself. Finally...

Never forget: **you are an officer** *of* **Marines.**

# Addenda

Here is a list of Internet resources you will find extraordinarily helpful as you prepare for OCS.  As a college student, you know you need more than one source to effectively synthesize concepts – and we know it, too.  We wrote this book to prepare you in the best way possible for OCS, but there are plenty of fantastic books, blogs, web sites, white papers, videos and more out there on the Web that you can supplement your preparations with.  Here are our recommendations:

**Cleaning the M16:**

The Army actually has an excellent study guide for maintaining and cleaning weapons that transfers over perfectly to the Marine Corps.  Check it out here:

http://www.armystudyguide.com/content/Prep_For_Basic_Training/prep_for_basic_common_tasks/maintain-an-m16a2-rifle.shtml

You can also watch a very thorough video on it here:

http://www.youtube.com/watch?v=_HXFobzhJdo

**Running the Combat Fitness Test**

There is an excellent video of Marines conducting the CFT (very quickly and competently) on YouTube.  This course is designed to break you off, so be ready for it.  Watch it here:

http://www.youtube.com/watch?v=eBgdPT2A_Lw

**Excellent Preparatory Resources for OCS**

If you are anything like the authors of this book and didn't even see *Full Metal Jacket* before you chose to try joining the Marines, you should get an introduction to your chosen branch of service before shipping off to Quantico.  This PBS documentary is one of the best:

http://www.youtube.com/watch?v=vPg2Kf-jYeA

You can also read an excellent book called "One Bullet Away: The Making of a Marine Officer" which will help you with a lot of context and advice.  You can purchase it at Amazon here:

http://www.amazon.com/One-Bullet-Away-Making-Officer/dp/B002ECETVS

If you want a good chuckle, but also to gain a little inside perspective of the attitude and ethos of the USMC, be sure to check out Terminal Lance at http://www.terminallance.com

19785217R00074

Made in the USA
Middletown, DE
03 May 2015